GOOD KARMA

GOOD KARMA

HOW TO FIND IT AND KEEP IT

JOAN DUNCAN OLIVER

dbp

DUNCAN BAIRD PUBLISHERS

LONDON

Good Karma
Joan Duncan Oliver

Distributed in the USA and Canada by
Sterling Publishing Co., Inc.
387 Park Avenue South
New York, NY 10016-8810

This edition first published in the UK and USA in 2006 by
Duncan Baird Publishers Ltd
Sixth Floor, Castle House
75–76 Wells Street
London W1T 3QH

Managing Designer: Daniel Sturges
Commissioned illustrations: Asami Matsuhira at 3+Co.

Library of Congress Cataloging-in-Publication
Data Available

ISBN-13: 978-1-84483-323-8
ISBN-10: 1-84483-323-2
10 9 8 7 6 5 4 3

Typeset in Frutiger and MrsEaves
Color reproduction by Colourscan, Singapore
Printed in Singapore

For information about custom editions, special sales,
premium and corporate purchases, please contact
Sterling Special Sales Department at 800-805-5489
or specialsales@sterlingpub.com.

The abbreviations BCE and CE are used throughout
this book. BCE means Before the Common Era
(equivalent to BC); CE means Of the Common Era
(equivalent to AD).

Contents

Introduction

Karma. Pop stars, rockers, and rappers from John Lennon and XTC to Lloyd Banks and Alicia Keys have recorded songs on the subject. "Was it something I did in another life?" Warren Zevon mused in *Bad Karma*. "Ain't no running from karma," warned the Black Eyed Peas. Even primetime TV has taken up the karma theme. In a situation comedy about a guy who set out to make amends for all the bad things he'd done, the lead character crowed, "There's something to be said for waking up and feeling like a good person." Indeed.

The Buddha might have had a thing or two to say about the way karma has entered our culture—with scarcely a nod to the profound teachings that underlie the concept. But even for those schooled in its doctrinal origins, how karma plays out in everyday life can seem maddeningly elusive. The Buddha himself called karma one of the "four unconjecturables," meaning we could drive ourselves nuts speculating on the way it might unfold over time.

What is karma anyway? Probably not what you think. It's not fate, or the provider of parking spaces, or a cosmic reward for seemly conduct. Karma is the law of cause-and-effect operating in our actions and their results. Though the notion of karma originated in ancient India, every spiritual tradition from

Christianity to Wicca teaches some variation on the maxim "As ye sow, so shall ye reap." Ultimately, karma transcends religion, residing in the realm of perennial philosophy. Everyone seems to have a visceral sense of it: bikers and blue-haired grannies alike bat the term around in conversation. "What goes around, comes around," we whisper knowingly when word gets out that the town gossip has received a taste of her own.

But karma is not just some sort of cosmic charm school, pronouncing on good versus bad behavior. It's the glue holding humanity together, felt across the world. In a society of hermits, karma would be irrelevant, some have claimed. Who hasn't done something selfish or even illicit when she thought no one else was likely to find out? Alone in our rooms, we persuade ourselves we're beyond karma's force field. Karma comes alive in community. When we realize that our motives and actions are always open to scrutiny—whether by our fellows, a higher authority, or our own inner critic—the world is suddenly filled with moral choices. "When a man appears before the Throne of Judgment," the Talmud says, "the first question he is asked is not, 'Have you believed in God?' or 'Have you prayed and performed ritual acts?' but 'Have you dealt honorably, faithfully in all your dealings with your fellow man?'"

Though the idea of sin and redemption is particularly Western, in the East, too, we find rules for an upright life. To Hindus, karma is associated with duty—

fulfilling one's obligations means fulfilling one's destiny. But even within the guidelines of philosophy and religion, there's plenty of room to maneuver. It's called free will. The strictest moralist must make choices.

It's these choices that concern us here. In our multicultural, multidimensional, increasingly complex world, how can we live in harmony with ourselves and with each other? How do we decide what's right and fair, and pattern our behavior accordingly? And given the sorry state of everything from basic manners to global diplomacy, how can we shape ourselves and our offspring into people of integrity with the wisdom and compassion not to blow up the planet?

Sounds like a tall order, but when we look closer, we see that this challenge isn't peculiar to our times, it's an age-old quest. As citizens of the 21st century, we're blessed with thousands of years of human success and failure to consult in making the decisions and adjustments that will affect human happiness and well-being for today, tomorrow, and generations— even lifetimes—to come.

Yes, lifetimes. Traditionally, reincarnation is the central idea underpinning the workings of karma. A belief that this lifetime is neither our first nor, in all likelihood, our last puts our behavior as individuals in perspective and impels us to be responsible in all our interactions. Even non-believers concede the benefits of taking others into account.

This book contains twenty conversations on karma between a hypothetical seeker and a more seasoned voice. The dialogues are imagined, but any resemblance to discussions you might engage in is intentional. What we're grappling with in these pages are the kind of moral choices all of us are called on constantly to make—everyday ethics, in other words. Even for strict adherents of one code or another, life is full of situations that invite a reconsideration of the way things are done. Your personal experience may differ from the examples presented here, but we hope that the topics explored will provoke thought on matters of concern to us all.

Students of Eastern philosophy might see a contradiction in suggesting ways to acquire—and keep—good karma. Even though good karma is obviously preferable to bad, the goal of spiritual practice is to have *no* karma. To be free of karma means to be free of the angst and desire that bind us to the everyday world of cause-and-effect the Buddhists call "the wheel of *samsara*."

But that's for later. For now, our challenge is to develop the understanding, self-mastery, and compassion to behave in ways likely to create positive karma, and to avoid doing what's likely to produce its opposite. We're not gods, so we'll trip and fall. But with some grasp of how karma works, we can begin to see that "our life is not a series of random, insignificant, disconnected events," as the Buddhist teacher Reginald Ray has put it. "Anything that we do is meaningful, one way or another," he points out. "So don't waste your day."

WHAT IS KARMA?

How to live with the law of cause-and-effect

Karma is an ancient teaching of the East, though every culture has its own version of the adage "As ye sow, shall ye reap." What are the origins of karma? What do we mean when we use the term today? Briefly, here's how the law of consequences works.

Karma is a Sanskrit word meaning "action," though it's often used to refer to both an action and its results. Many people think of karma as Newton's Third Law—"For every action, there's an equal and opposite reaction"—as it applies to the psychological or ethical domain. Karma isn't luck or destiny—luck suggests randomness; destiny, a lack of choice. Nor is it the voice of the gods trying to keep us in line. Karma is a description of how moral law operates, not a prescription for good behavior. "Karma provides the stimulus, not the response to the situation," *The Encyclopedia of Eastern Philosophy and Religion* tells us.

Karma is a fundamental principle of Eastern philosophy, found in the Hindu, Buddhist, Jain, and Sikh traditions. It was first mentioned in the Vedas and Upanishads—early Hindu scriptures setting out the relationship between karma and virtuous conduct. Later, the Buddha refined the teachings, emphasizing volitional behavior and responsibility: we are the choices we make. Though karma originated in the East, the principle of cause-and-effect is universal. Consider this well-known passage from the New Testament, Galatians 6:

"WHERE A MAN SOWS, THERE HE REAPS. IF HE SOWS IN THE FIELD OF SELF-INDULGENCE HE WILL GET A HARVEST OF CORRUPTION ... IF HE SOWS IN THE FIELD OF THE SPIRIT HE WILL GET FROM IT A HARVEST OF ETERNAL LIFE."

Not unlike the Buddha's words: "Whatever I do, for good or for evil, to that I will fall heir ..."

But bad things happen to good people, too. Are you saying they're to blame?

There are no accidents, the law of karma tells us. But we're not the sole cause of our experience either:

many other factors usually contribute. Still, when terrible things happen to the undeserving we naturally search for reasons. Karma offers one explanation. Even the unimaginable can be rationalized through the lens of reincarnation. According to this doctrine, the soul or consciousness evolves over multiple lifetimes, all the while amassing karma arising from thoughts, words, and deeds. Karma not "cleared" in one incarnation is carried over to the next. "Whatever is in his mind at the time of death ... only that he becomes," the *Bhagavad-Gita* says. Today's victim may be paying for yesterday's misdeeds.

I don't buy this reincarnation business. It's so deterministic: whatever karma we're born with preordains our fate.

On the contrary. Free will is integral to karma. Without free will, change would be impossible. Hindu texts describe three types of karma. Only one— *prarabdha karma*—is unchangeable. The portion of our accumulated karma that is ripenening in this lifetime, it determines the circumstances of our birth and our genetic inheritance. The remaining stored karma— *samchita karma*, which reveals itself in our habits and tendencies—can to some extent be altered by our efforts, as can *agami karma*—future karma we're now creating. How we work with karma defines our character.

As the Theravada Buddhist teacher Mahasi Sayadaw explained:

"WE ARE AT LIBERTY TO CREATE FRESH KARMA THAT LEADS TOWARD EITHER OUR PROGRESS OR OUR DOWNFALL."

Is the goal to avoid creating negative karma we might have to drag around for years or even lifetimes?

We can't avoid creating karma. Every action has effects. But we can do our best to cause no harm and to behave in ways that are likely to generate positive karma or transform bad karma into good. The ultimate goal, according to the traditional teachings, isn't to store up good karma but to get rid of *all* karma. Enlightened beings are said to be happy and at peace because they're free of the confusion,

fears, and appetites that keep us dashing this way
and that, never satisfied, lifetime after lifetime.

*I can see how someone steeped in Eastern philosophy might relate to
this view, but what about the rest of us?*

Every religion and philosophical system has some
form of ethics—a set of standards or code of conduct
by which to live. Depending on your beliefs, "right
behavior" might mean adhering to commandments
handed down by divine decree, or guidelines derived
from other sacred or secular teachings. Buddhism is a
non-theistic philosophy: its adherents follow precepts
grounded in principles of non-harming that the
Buddha perceived directly at the time of his great
awakening. In Christianity, Judaism, and Islam, right
action has a strong moral dimension: going against
God's will is a sin. Sinning is analogous to behavior
that produces karma—do wrong and there will be
negative consequences.

The Abrahamic religions hold that sin can be
erased by God's grace, here or in the hereafter. But
for Buddhists, there is no divine force meting out
reward and punishment, no Judgment Day or
heavenly reprieve—only the inexorable force of

karma. "Work out your own salvation with diligence," the Buddha told his followers. We create
our own karma and by our own efforts surmount it.

*When people say things like "I've got bad relationship karma,"
they're not talking about sin. What is karma in that context?*

To some people karma is psychological baggage—a
fear of intimacy, say—that needs to be resolved,
while others see it as an ethical matter: What is
likely to do the most good—or the least harm—in
this situation? Here, the focus is on intention: are
you operating from your nobler instincts—courtesy,

> According to the seed that's
> sown, so is the fruit you reap
> therefrom.
> Doer of good will gather good.
> Doer of evil, evil reaps ...

SAMYUTTA NIKAYA

compassion, wisdom—or is your behavior shortsighted and selfishly motivated? Karma functions as an efficient early-warning system.

Put that way, karma sounds like a general guide to right living.

Definitely. Karma appears in many guises. Native Americans make decisions for "the seventh generation": with an eye to the consequences for people seven generations hence and, by default, for everyone born in the meantime. Karma restores balance in the world.

Neopagans and Wiccans cleave to the Threefold Law, or Law of Return, which holds that both the good and harm we do will rebound to us. Karma as "the unerring Law of Retribution" also figures prominently in Theosophy, the esoteric system introduced to the West by the mystic Helena Blavatsky, as well as in many New Age teachings.

Even the 19th-century Transcendentalist Ralph Waldo Emerson seems to have channeled age-old teachings on karma in his essay *Compensation*: "You cannot do wrong without suffering wrong ... on the other hand, the law holds with equal sureness for all right action. Love, and you shall be loved."

SETTING
YOUR DESTINY

How to know when you have choices

The law of karma is paradoxical. It says we're responsible for our actions but not necessarily in control of the outcome. How can that be? When we explore the nuances of accountability and free will, we learn that our destiny turns less on what happens to us than on how we handle it.

I seesaw between believing we create our own reality and thinking external forces must be pulling the strings. To what degree are we responsible for our circumstances? How much control do we really have in life?

That's the big question: Who's in charge here? If we believe that an all-powerful force—God, divine energy, natural law—determines our every move, we'll always be at the mercy of some sort of cosmic justice system: If we're good, life is good; if we misbehave, bad things happen. But experience tells us that's not how it works. Bad things happen to good people and vice versa.

Is that where karma comes in—my baggage from the past defines my life going forward?

Karma isn't that deterministic. The law of karma simply says that every action has a consequence. What happened in the past brought us to the present moment, but what happens from here isn't set in stone. We have choices. That's the variable—free will. As the authors of our own experience, we have a lot of latitude. To that extent, we're accountable for our dramas, for creating our own heaven and hell. Our choices influence the course of our daily lives. But it's important to make a distinction between responsibility and control. We're in charge of our responses—what we say and do—but beyond that we can't guarantee the outcome. We may aim for a certain result, but we can't be sure we'll hit the mark. Countless other factors and forces are at work in every situation. Most we're not even aware of.

I can see how I contribute to what happens in my personal life. But are you suggesting that we're responsible for the big, impersonal things, too—wars, the weather, natural disasters?

Of course not. We can't even *predict* the weather with total accuracy, never mind control it. But this doesn't mean we should beg off responsibility in all cases. Are you using your vote to express your stance on war, for example? Some would even argue we play a role in natural disasters: as consumers we contribute to global warming, which is a factor in the climate shifts causing cataclysmic storms. And what about taking responsibility for your choices? If you buy a house on a flood plain or fault line, are you prepared to face the consequences?

Are you saying that we bring difficulties on ourselves?

Not necessarily. Not everyone has a range of choices.

The poor in particular are often trapped by circumstances. They may lack the resources to live in safe areas or evacuate in the event of disaster.

So where does karma fit in here? After the tsunami of 2004, I asked a friend how she could bear the pain of knowing so many people had lost so much. "I just remember it's their karma," she said. Her reply seemed so callous, but is this how karma works?

Most of us feel sorrow and compassion in response to human tragedy. That's what prompts us to reach out and help. Unfortunately, a fatalistic view like your friend's is often used to rationalize not taking action on behalf of those who are suffering. The excuse usually runs something like this: "We shouldn't interfere because these people have a spiritual lesson to learn"—some personal issue to work out or karmic debt to pay. The corollary to that is even more invidious: "They brought it on themselves and are just getting what they deserved."

But before you judge your friend too harshly, consider the possibility that her words mask something deeper—fear, perhaps, or a feeling of helplessness. Heartless as it seems, "blaming the victim" is the only way some people can cope when they're overwhelmed by strong emotions.

So I shouldn't confront my friend about her response?

By all means speak up, if you're moved to. Your friend may not even realize how uncaring she sounds. But try not to be judgmental. Instead, use the occasion to discuss what karma really means and the nature of our responsibility toward others. A frank but caring conversation could open your friend's eyes to the world's suffering—and open your own heart to the pain she's experiencing.

I'm never sure when to jump in or back off. Don't we all have our own karma?

If the house were on fire, you wouldn't wonder whether to help people find the exit. In emergencies we act without thought to karmic implications. The rest of the time, we can weigh the consequences before stepping in. Whenever I take on some aspect of your life, I'm influencing your karma, as well as my own. Maybe you're a dunce with money, so I give you cash. That gets you out of debt and cleans up your credit. That's good. But I haven't helped you learn how to manage your finances so you can stay out of debt. Maybe you need to work that out on your own. So, on balance, will my intervention be helpful or harmful? We may not know right away. Often the fruits of karma don't appear for years—or lifetimes. Therefore, our responsibility is to be very conscious—and conscientious—in whatever we decide to do.

With so many forces in play, how much choice do we have about who we are and how we live?

Our genes determine our physical appearance and influence our emotional makeup. And if you believe in rebirth, you can add the accrued experience of past lifetimes to your inborn endowment. But even if it feels as if you're constrained by past and present circumstances, every minute of the day you're making choices: for or against, this or that, yes or no. Each choice reshapes you, for better or worse. Your brain and your character are constantly evolving. Karma doesn't move in a straight line from past to future. The Buddha likened the process to flowing water. Thanissaro Bhikkhu, a Theravada Buddhist monk in the Thai forest tradition, has explained it nicely: "Sometimes the flow from the past is so strong that little can be done except to stand fast, but there are

" No snowflake in an avalanche ever feels responsible. "

VOLTAIRE (1694–1778)

also times when the flow is gentle enough to be diverted in almost any direction."

Still, I often feel at the mercy of circumstances. My boss has expectations I have to meet to keep my job. My family has its own demands. Though I practice meditation, I still lose my temper now and then. Even my bank balance dictates how I live. Where's the freedom in all that?

Free will only means choice, it doesn't put you in charge of circumstances. You can't, for example, foresee that your neighbor will drive his car over your front lawn or that your nephew will suddenly turn up at your door with his backpack. Even your inner experience isn't completely under your control: thoughts and emotions bubble up unbidden.

Again, your choice is in your response. You can go after your neighbor with a tire iron, or else you can invite him over to help you re-sod the lawn. You can simmer in silence while your nephew makes himself at home, or you can give him a ride to the nearest youth hostel.

So are you saying I'm responsible for my destiny after all?

You're responsible for showing up for life—for being aware and taking decisions and actions as required; for learning right from wrong and behaving accordingly; and for taking care of yourself and those who depend on you.

THINGS WON'T ALWAYS TURN OUT AS YOU HOPED OR PLANNED, BUT IF YOU SEIZE OPPORTUNITIES, ACT DILIGENTLY AND FAIRLY, AND SHOW GOODWILL TOWARD OTHERS, YOU'LL ENJOY A FULL, RICH LIFE, UNBURDENED BY REGRETS.

MAKING THE RIGHT DECISIONS

How your motives shape your life

*"As ye sow, shall ye reap." Intention plants
the seeds of the life we lead. When our motives
are pure, the karmic fruits are nourishing.
When we sow carelessness, duplicity, or ill
will, sorrow and disappointment are the
likely yield. We are only as happy as the
choices we make.*

I'm still confused about how karma works. Does it matter what I do if I don't mean any harm, or if I don't know that I'm doing anything wrong?

Buddhist teachings say that karma arises from *volitional* words and deeds—the conscious choices we make. We're not accountable for unconscious or involuntary actions—the beating of your heart doesn't produce karma, though a heart attack might, if you've been careless about your health. Ignorance, too, may get us off the hook karmically speaking, if not in the eyes of the law. Everyone makes mistakes, and a code of conduct that didn't allow for an unintentional misstep now and then wouldn't be much help for getting on in the world. Thoughts arise in our minds unbidden; that in itself doesn't generate karma. But how and where we direct those thoughts shapes our lives.

So what about the old saw, "The road to hell is paved with good intentions"? That seems to be saying that intentions aren't important, what matters is the outcome.

If karma were deterministic, we wouldn't give intention much thought. Whatever we did, good or bad, would be rewarded in kind. But karma doesn't

> **" Promise only what you can deliver. Then deliver more than you promise. "**
>
> ANONYMOUS

work that way. It isn't linear, and it doesn't yield its fruits on a timetable. We can't say, "If I do x today, I'll get y result tomorrow." Karmically speaking, we're living simultaneously in three time zones—the past, the present, and the future—as T.S. Eliot pointed out so eloquently in his poem "Burnt Norton," from *Four Quartets*. While we can't help bringing the events of the past—even the imprint of what might have happened but didn't—into the present, we have some choice about what happens from here. To a large extent we shape the future, in other words. That's why intention is so important. We can't say for certain how life will play out, but we have a better shot at happy endings if our motivation is sincere.

But what about those times when I think I'm doing the right thing, but the results aren't so hot?

Thanissaro Bhikkhu, a Theravada Buddhist monk in the Thai forest tradition, addresses that point:

"NOT ALL GOOD INTENTIONS ARE ESPECIALLY SKILLFUL. EVEN THOUGH THEY MEAN WELL, THEY CAN BE MISGUIDED AND INAPPROPRIATE FOR THE OCCASION, THUS RESULTING IN PAIN AND REGRET."

Could that be what happened to my friend? She decided not to tell her family she was undergoing an extensive, debilitating medical treatment, and when they found out, they were furious. Her father was so hurt he refused to talk to her. Her sister was annoyed at being thrust into the role of go-between. Meanwhile, my friend lost the support of her family at a critical time.

That's a good example of what happens when our intentions are good but our methods aren't sound. In our desire to spare people worry, we may fail to think through how they will perceive what we do. The smallest decision can have a seismic effect if we're not mindful in our approach to the situation.

Another way intention can derail us, Thanissaro Bhikku says, is if we fail to realize that our good intentions are, in reality, mixed. Let's say you've always been kind and attentive to your grandmother, so after her death you're stunned to find out she barely mentioned you in her will. If you examine your motives closely, however, you may see that although no one could deny you were a dutiful granddaughter, you also had your inheritance on your mind.

But don't we usually have mixed motives? In fact, I am close to my grandmother, but sometimes I'm resentful when her needs interfere with my plans, like the weekend I had to cancel a trip so I could put up her screens. Where does that leave me in terms of karma?

Only time will tell. That's why we need to live impeccably, with full awareness that any action can produce results at any time. One thing karma does is act as a deterrent. If we don't want to risk having something undesirable happen, we're likely to give more thought to the consequences of what we say and do.

So something like keeping a promise would be really important?

Absolutely. Promises and trust go hand in hand. And trust is fundamental to interpersonal relations. We trust that other people won't harm us and will be as good as their word. If we can't trust anyone, life becomes hell on earth. People with paranoid tendencies are miserable, always assuming the worst of those around them and never feeling they're on stable ground. Just as a promissory note signifies an intention to pay a debt, a promise signifies an intention to do what we say, whether it's to keep a confidence, honor a deal, or meet a friend for dinner.

What if I break a promise?

There are bound to be ramifications. By your actions you've announced that you're not trustworthy. People will stop confiding in you, which means you'll lose a degree of intimacy and miss out on vital information. They'll stop assuming you'll keep your word, which will affect your relationships and maybe even your livelihood. Your boss and co-workers will question whether you can be relied on to carry out an assignment or close a sale.

But what if circumstances change? Is a promise binding then? I promised my father we'd never put him in a home, but as his Alzheimer's advanced a special facility was the only place that could give him the right care.

Alzheimer's disease is challenging for even professionals to deal with. You're to be applauded for getting your father the best care you could find. If your intention was loving, you can rest easy. But if you stashed him there simply because his behavior was getting on your nerves, at some point you're likely to reap the fruits of your selfishness, if only to feel guilty that you let him down.

There will always be exceptions, as you've discovered. But in general, it's best to keep promises. People will feel safe with you and will know they can count on you. That's karmic gold in the bank.

What if my intentions are above reproach and I take the right action, but still I get negative results? What's going on here?

You know how I said we couldn't always predict when and how karma would come back to us? A negative outcome in the present may be fallout from an unwise decision in the past. Let's say you're raising money to renovate housing for the homeless, and you go to see a potential funder. The cause is worthy, the funder is sympathetic, and your pitch strikes just the right note. Still, she turns you down. You're at a loss to explain why. Then you remember that back in your rebellious youth, you and some friends lobbed firecrackers onto her lawn, scorching the bushes and scaring her dachshund. Just your luck she has a long memory. But all is not lost. You'll have to redouble your efforts to secure funding, but karma has presented you with a chance to make amends.

"Happy is the person whose karma is his *dharma*"—his path—the Islamic scholar Seyyed Hossein Nasr has said. Karma brings us the lessons we need to learn and the messes we need to tidy up. It calls us to reset our intentions and bring forth the best we have to offer.

DISCOVERING
THE TRUE YOU

How to make the most of who you are

Are you ready to emerge from the cocoon of your past? The key to inner freedom is self-reflection—uncovering the habits that have held you back and identifying your strong points. With self-knowledge comes the ability to frame new responses and to relate authentically to the world.

Lately, whenever I try to start something new, whether it's a project or a friendship, things don't seem to come together as I'd hoped or planned. I make all the right moves, but success remains elusive. Somebody suggested that the problem is something I'm not looking at—a hidden assumption I'll fail, for example. Maybe so, but I don't see how digging around in my psyche will help. I simply want to get on with my life. Any suggestions?

Unfortunately, we can't just set aside what we don't want to think about and assume that it will go away. Whoever suggested you try a little self-exploration makes a good point. When we've exhausted all the excuses for why life isn't working—other people, bad luck, misalignment of the stars—we're left with the possibility that the answer lies within. Nine times out of ten, it's our fears or doubts or attitudes— carryovers from the past—that are getting in the way of our accomplishing what we want.

Can't I just let bygones be bygones and start afresh?

Unfortunately, "the eternal sunshine of the spotless mind" exists only in the movies. Even if you could ignore the past, I doubt that would make you happy. The past is the repository of *all* your experiences—the joys and triumphs, as well as the disappointments.

Without your past, you wouldn't be you. When you say you want to put it behind you, don't you mean you want to be free of unpleasant memories?

I guess so. Whenever I think about the past, I have a thousand regrets. Every "Why did I ...?" or "Why didn't I ..." feels like karmic punishment for my sins.

Everyone has regrets. We've all said or done things we're not proud of, or that failed to get us the results we want. But torturing yourself by rehashing those moments isn't going to put the past to rest any more than ignoring them would. Karma isn't a cosmic evaluation slip that says, "Too bad, you failed the test." It's merely a clue to where you need to do some self-reflection. Karma says,

MINE YOUR EXPERIENCE FOR WHAT IT CAN TEACH YOU ABOUT YOUR HABITUAL RESPONSES TO THE WORLD.

You need to find out what's keeping you from expressing fully who you are.

If I look, I'll only feel inadequate. Maybe whatever is happening now is just my karma, and the best I can do is accept it.

There's a common misconception that karma locks us into what was true in the past. Fortunately, that's not the case. Character and personality are malleable. We can and do change. In fact, our inner experience of the world changes constantly. That's why it matters so much what thoughts we entertain. If we cling to our old ways of thinking, we'll simply respond as we always have and the same things will keep happening to us. The first step toward awakening is admitting you want something different.

Since things aren't going my way right now, I suppose my whole life could use an overhaul.

It isn't a matter of overhauling your life—though aspects of your life are bound to change as you develop self-awareness. This is about understanding who you are at the core. We all have within us a wealth of resources—everything, in fact, we need for growth. Evolution has seen to that. The way to tap that inner wisdom is through self-examination.

Self-examination is fine in theory, but how do I find time for it?
I'm already juggling the demands of family, work, and community.
I can barely squeeze in twenty minutes of yoga as it is.

Developing insight isn't just one more obligation to jam into an already crowded schedule. It's a shift in focus, a different way of looking at yourself. If you want to break the bonds of karma, you have to make self-awareness a priority.

That sounds pretty self-indulgent—a solipsistic obsession with the Great Me.

Hardly. The quest for self-knowledge is the oldest quest on earth. No sooner had man discovered fire than he probably asked himself,

"WHO AM I? WHY AM I HERE? HOW SHOULD I LIVE?"

These aren't just questions for the intellect to mull over. They push you to look closely at how you define yourself. Are you a person you admire? Are you living according to what matters most to you? Character and karma are intertwined.

How so?

The roles you identify with are reflected in how your life plays out. If, say, you're caught up in the role of entrepreneur and launching a new venture, your world will consist of bankers, business plans, and marketing opportunities. That in turn will ramp up your ambition and your anxiety about succeeding— qualities you'll feed back into the fledgling enterprise as heightened pressure to make good. Gradually your focus will narrow till everything and everyone you encounter is somehow related to your goal. Ideally, you would then stop and ask yourself: *Is this the person I want to be? Is what I'm doing consistent with my values?*

But who's going to stop for that kind of self-reflection?

In fact, self-reflection is very practical. What are the hopes and dreams you cherish, the abilities you aren't yet actualizing? What are the secrets and nasty little habits you're hiding? Only if you bring all this to light will you be able to lead the full, rich life you crave.

So I've got to own all my "stuff"—even what I'm afraid to see?

> **People travel to wonder at the height of mountains, at the huge waves of the sea, at the long courses of rivers, at the vast compass of the ocean, at the circular motion of the stars; and they pass themselves without wondering.**
>
> SAINT AUGUSTINE (354–430 CE)

Especially what you're afraid to see. To break the cycle of karma, you have to break the cycle of unskillful behavior. You can't keep saying and doing the same things and expect better results. When you see your behavior clearly you can frame new responses. There are many techniques for increasing self-awareness. Most involve mindfulness—observing what's happening in the present moment: your thoughts, emotions, and bodily sensations.

I see how mindfulness could enhance my experience of the present, but how will it help me put the past to rest?

The only place you can change the past is in the present. By not focusing on the "story" of your life—the events themselves—but rather on how you interpret and shape those events, you will start to see patterns emerging. Insight into the assumptions that have been running your life will tell you why things turn out in certain ways. The patterns and habits you've developed are karmic opportunities. Unlike age or eye color or family of origin, they're aspects of yourself you have the power to change, which could, in turn, change your life. Karma arises out of our choices. When we choose not to respond as in the past, we create the possibility of a different future. Virginia Woolf wrote:

"THE MAN WHO IS AWARE OF HIMSELF IS HENCEFORWARD INDEPENDENT, AND HE IS NEVER BORED."

LIVING
PASSIONATELY

How to deal skillfully with your feelings

Emotions give life texture and depth, but there's an art to managing our moods. Once we cultivate inner balance we can immerse ourselves fully in every experience without fear of going overboard. When we're conversant with our emotions, we learn to nurture positive feelings and defuse disturbing ones.

My friends say I'm too emotional. True, I feel things deeply—others'
pain as much as my own. But I don't see the problem. Isn't it better
to be responsive than remote and unfeeling?

> Being emotionally attuned to other people is a
> wonderful quality. We could use more empathy in the
> world. You can't resonate with others' feelings unless
> you're in touch with your own. But when you let
> your emotions run away with you, you're unlikely to
> get the results you want. We all know the force of
> anger, jealousy, and other destructive emotions. But
> even positive emotions like love and joy can lead to
> sorrow if we try to make them last forever. All the
> wisdom teachings emphasize moderation as the way
> to inner balance.

"Inner balance" sounds so boring. Can't we be passionately engaged
in life without leaving destruction in our wake?

> Absolutely. No one's suggesting you take a vow of
> emotional austerity. Besides, even if you wanted to,
> you couldn't stop emotions from arising: they're part
> of your essential makeup.

Negative emotions, too?

> There's some disagreement on that. Buddhists, for
> example, say that our basic nature is free of anger,

> " It is not what **happens** to us that **disturbs** us, but what we **think** about what happens to us. "
>
> EPICTETUS (55–C.135 CE)

envy, fear, and other afflictive emotions. Western psychology, on the other hand, holds that negative emotions are inherently human and the best we can do is learn to handle them with skill. Even Buddhists generally agree that getting rid of destructive emotions altogether is a tall order that only the most advanced spiritual practitioners achieve. The Dalai Lama admits he gets angry at times, and not long ago I heard him say with a laugh that he's jealous of his translator's "beautiful English." Of course, His Holiness is a lot more attuned to his mind states than most people and can let go of anger and jealousy as they arise. For the rest of us, recognizing and managing our emotions so they don't manage us is a worthy goal.

*But emotions arise so quickly. Even before I realize I'm angry,
I've lost my temper, it seems. How can I possibly manage that?*

Emotions seem to seize us without warning. "We
only become aware once we're in the emotion,"
psychologist Paul Ekman has pointed out.

"WE'RE NOT THE MASTER AT THE START."

Once we're in the thrall of an emotion—a negative
one, at least—reasoning and impulse control rapidly
decline. It's hard not to do or say something we'll
later regret. We need to sharpen our awareness of
how emotions arise so we can identify those points in
the process when it's possible to intervene.

So I'd be able to suppress a painful emotion like anger or envy?

Suppressing an emotion doesn't work. Put any
volatile substance under extreme pressure and it's
bound to explode. The simplest way to learn about
negative emotions is by reflecting on them after the
fact: Did you express the emotion or exercise

restraint? What was the outcome? How could you ensure a more favorable result in the future? As you refine your awareness, the next step is to catch emotions as they arise. Then you can weigh the consequences before you plunge into action. Admittedly, it's hard to be reflective in the throes of emotion. But if you keep at it you'll see something interesting happen. Take anger. If you can investigate it without obsessively rehashing the incident, not only will you learn about what ticks you off but the anger itself will start to dissipate. As Matthieu Richard, a Tibetan Buddhist monk, explains: "The more you look at anger, the more it disappears ... like the frost melting under the morning sun."

Are you suggesting I'll have the presence of mind to sit down in the middle of an anger attack and meditate? I don't think so. I need a method I can use on the fly.

Emotions register in the body long before we're conscious of them. You can mentally scan your body for where there's tension, then breathe into those spots to release it. As your body relaxes, the emotion will ease its grip.

Another method for managing emotions is to

replace a disturbing feeling with a positive one. You can't feel two opposing emotions at once. So if you're angry, focus on love. If you envy someone, imagine feeling pleasure at their good fortune. It helps to keep an inspiring verse handy for reflection. Try the prayer attributed to Saint Francis of Assisi:

"LORD, MAKE ME A CHANNEL OF THY PEACE THAT WHERE THERE IS HATRED, I MAY BRING LOVE ... THAT WHERE THERE IS DISCORD, I MAY BRING HARMONY ... THAT WHERE THERE IS SADNESS, I MAY BRING JOY. ..."

To restore calm when you're agitated, meditation is helpful. As you become more at home with the shifts and shadings of your emotions, you will be less reactive.

I can see how those techniques would help me hold my temper, but what if there's a legitimate reason to be angry?

So-called "justifiable anger" can be tricky. Think of the last time you let fly at someone. Did it bring you closer? Things said or done in the heat of the moment may reverberate for years, causing damage to ourselves and people around us. It takes a high level of awareness to wield anger skillfully; most of us flunk the course. At the same time, we shouldn't shy away from examining our anger for the messages it brings us. As psychiatrist Mark Epstein explains,

"ANGER IS A SIGN THAT SOMETHING NEEDS TO CHANGE."

What about positive emotions? Isn't it good to express them when we can?

Definitely. Neuroscientists have found that when we experience emotions we lay down—or reinforce— tracks in the brain that make it easier to feel that way again. Emotions like love, compassion, and joy not only benefit *us* but are infectious. Remaining steady and loving in the face of negativity is one of the most effective ways to restore harmony and foster positive karma. Some years ago, Japanese Buddhist monks wanted to build a peace pagoda on a mountain overlooking a traditional New England town. Local residents initially opposed the project, but to everyone's surprise they came around. One townsperson told a newspaper reporter that the head monk's "ability to absorb their anger really changed people's hearts." We can all be like that monk.

How can I stay loving and positive all the time?

You can't. And if you tried, you'd only alienate yourself from your true feelings and other people.

EMOTIONS CHANGE. MOODS COME AND GO. ACCEPTING THIS OPENS THE DOOR TO A FULL, RICH, PASSIONATE LIFE.

Dialogue **6**

SHAPING YOUR REALITY

How to use your mind to change your karma

"You are what you think," we often hear. Our thoughts create our reality. Thoughts are the raw material from which we shape an identity, and the force behind what we say and do. Hardly a thought goes by without producing karma, so it's wise to make our thinking positive.

I'm starting to understand how our words and actions produce karma, but our thoughts? I don't buy it.

We'd like to believe that our thoughts are inconsequential, but the truth is just the opposite. "The thought is father to the deed," as the saying goes. Thoughts are the energy driving speech and action. Without thoughts there would be no karma.

But what about thoughts I keep to myself—that I don't put into words or action? Surely they're not causing any harm.

Don't bet on it. What you keep to yourself affects at least one person—you—and almost always has a wider impact. Our secret thoughts are seldom as innocent as we wish.

"NEVER SUFFER A THOUGHT TO BE HARBORED IN YOUR MIND WHICH YOU WOULD NOT AVOW OPENLY,"

Thomas Jefferson wrote in a letter to his grandson.

"When tempted to do anything in secret, ask yourself if you would do it in public. If you would not, be sure it is wrong." Hardly a moment goes by when we're not engaged in some sort of internal dialogue, rationalizing our behavior and beliefs. Want to test the notion that thoughts are insignificant if you keep them to yourself? Pick a recent incident in your life, and we'll see what you were thinking.

Here's one: The other morning it was raining and I was running late for work, so I hailed a taxi. Suddenly, a man darted in front of me and stole my cab. Needless to say, I was really annoyed and muttered a few choice words. I wasn't exactly wishing him well, I admit, but it's not as if he—or anyone else—could hear what I said. As I see it, no harm done.

Are you sure? Listen to your language. You say the

Judge no man until you have walked two moons in his moccasins.

NATIVE AMERICAN PROVERB

man "stole" your cab. Right away, you've made a judgment: he did something almost criminal—-that taxi was *yours*. And while you were standing there bristling with indignation, stress hormones were flooding your system, priming your brain for further vengeful thoughts. If, at that point, you'd shrugged off the incident, maybe no one but you would have been affected. But I'm guessing you didn't drop the matter there.

No. I kept replaying it in my head while I waited for the bus. And when the bus didn't come, my thoughts raced ahead to work: "See what that guy made me do? Now I'll never get to the office. The boss will be furious. I'll be in so much trouble. Maybe he'll even fire me."

What makes our thoughts harmful is not that they're negative—negative thoughts arise unbidden in our minds all the time—but that we don't stop at one. One thought leads to another and another until, like putting a match to a woodpile, we've ignited a raging fire. There you were slogging through the rain, stoking your anger as you rehashed what happened. As your mood darkened, it inevitably colored all your thoughts, even those unrelated to the taxi incident.

Some of those thoughts were bound to spill over into action. Maybe you snapped at a woman who grazed you with her umbrella, or tapped your fingers impatiently as the newsseller fumbled for change, or shot thunderous looks at a knot of school kids hogging the sidewalk. By then, you were radiating so much negativity you didn't have to say a word to disturb everyone you encountered. Our thoughts, far from being incidental, have such far-reaching potential that it raises the question of whether there's any such thing as a private thought.

That's a scary notion. What's the solution—to develop more willpower so I can control my thoughts?

Trying to control thoughts is like trying to corral wild monkeys. The goal isn't thought control but mind mastery—the ability to deal with whatever thoughts arise. The famous Zen master Shunryu Suzuki said the way to control a cow is to put it in a large pasture and watch what it does. Our minds are like the cow, he was suggesting. When we can let our thoughts come and go without obsessing on them or resisting them, we can gain enough perspective to make better choices. If you had been more alert to your mind state when the man took your cab, you might have been able to tell yourself, "I could lose my temper here, but it wouldn't help," then turned your attention to finding another way to get to work. You might even have had the presence of mind to call out, "Which way are you headed? OK if we share the cab?" A mind that isn't fixated on a certain outcome is open to creative solutions. If, as a last resort, you'd been able at some point to interrupt the volley of angry thoughts and say, "Enough—stop," you might have been able to put the incident behind you sooner, so it wouldn't have ruined your day.

But so often thoughts flood my mind before I have a chance to take hold of them. How can I stop runaway thinking?

Meditation and cognitive therapy offer techniques for interrupting the flow. If you sit quietly and examine your thoughts—Tibetan Buddhists call this "staring back"—you'll see that they have no substance, no permanence. Under scrutiny, thoughts dissolve. Cognitive therapy presupposes that harmful thoughts are errors in reasoning. Your first error was thinking that the cab belonged to you and therefore you were entitled to it. The second was thinking that the guy who took the cab had it in for you. Once you realize these assumptions are wrong, you can substitute more accurate ones: the cab belongs to the cab company and anyone is entitled to use it, and the man—like you—was only trying to get to work and probably didn't even see you hailing the taxi. Giving him the benefit of the doubt is an expansive thought that expresses your innate generosity and compassion. Thinking this way will make you feel better than if you assume the worst, and that will generate good karma.

So far you've been talking about negative thoughts, but aren't many of our thoughts positive ones that can benefit ourselves and others?

Absolutely. Constructive thoughts point us toward what's good for us and away from what's harmful. Our ability to reason leads to wise decisions and actions. A simple thought like "I want to look good at my high school reunion," or "My doctor says I need to lower my cholesterol," triggers more thoughts—"I need to lose 15 pounds"; "I owe it to my family to be healthy"—and soon you're forgoing dessert in favor of a trip to the gym. Thoughts allow us to plan for the future. When we're thinking straight we can channel our best intentions. Weighing the consequences before we dive in raises the probability of a positive outcome.

So all I have to do to change my life is change my thinking?

It's a start. Our thoughts have a lot to do with shaping our character and our experiences—and therefore our karma. If your thoughts are hostile, you'll experience the world as a dangerous place full of self-serving individuals, and you'll always be on the defensive. If you view the world through a kindlier, more hopeful lens, you'll experience it as a land of opportunity and well-intentioned people. "As [a man] thinketh in his heart, so is he," the Old Testament says. Our thoughts sometimes get us into trouble, but they're also our guides to a loving and productive life and better karma.

" The best thing to do when it's raining is to let it rain. "

HENRY WADSWORTH LONGFELLOW (1807–1882)

CREATING POSITIVE
RELATIONSHIPS

How to forge a positive bond

*"What goes around, comes around" is never
more evident than in intimate relations. Were
you brought together to resolve something
from the past? Whether or not a relationship
was preordained, it offers you a chance to
create a strong partnership and work out
your karma together in a loving way.*

*My friend insists we choose our intimate partners primarily for
one reason—we have karma from a previous lifetime to work out
together. Sometimes I think she might be right: certain issues keep
cropping up in my relationships. But is karma the explanation?*

Some traditional teachings might say so, but it would
be hard to prove. I wouldn't waste time running to
psychics for an answer. It would be far more practical
and profitable to consider what a relationship can
show you about how you're dealing with intimacy
in *this* lifetime. It's a safe assumption that when
something or someone stirs you up, there's a
problem you need to resolve. Whether you see it
as a habit pattern that isn't serving you or a karmic
knot to untangle is beside the point. We should
bless the people who arouse intense feelings in
us—they're potent teachers. If you can learn to see
yourself through others' eyes, you'll discover a lot
about the deeply ingrained ways of thinking that
drive your speech and actions.

How will that help me create closer relationships?

You mentioned you'd noticed certain recurring
patterns. That's an obvious place to start. Here's your
opportunity to work out destructive behavior that

may have plagued you for years. You don't have to announce to your partner, "I think we were enemies in a past life, and therefore we now have anger issues to resolve." Not everyone will share that view. Instead, simply pay attention when you find yourself in a familiar struggle. Notice what feelings are triggered, how you respond, and how the other person responds to you.

IF YOU CAN OBSERVE A PATTERN INSTEAD OF ACTING IT OUT IN A HARMFUL MANNER, IN TIME YOU'LL BE ABLE TO BREAK YOUR ATTACHMENT TO NEGATIVE WAYS OF REACTING AND FORM A MORE LOVING BOND WITH YOUR PARTNER.

Then my friend was right in saying that love relationships are about dealing with karma?

Karma colors all our relationships, not just intimate ones. But close relationships in particular call out the best and worst in us. Intimacy is a prime karmic breeding ground.

How can we tell whose karma is whose in a relationship? Are they separate—his, mine, and ours?

Both you and your partner come to the relationship with your own karmic baggage—your needs, wants, and emotional habits, as well as unresolved hurts and resentments from the past. Together you create a third entity—the relationship—that has its own identity and karma.

You mean relationship karma is different from the karma of the individual partners?

The karma of a relationship reflects both the strengths and weaknesses of what you're building together. To some extent it's influenced by your individual karma, as well as the collective karma of the time and place in which you live. Relationship karma is like a joint bank account. One partner might have a personal account that's always balanced to the penny, while the other's account is always in arrears. But their joint account may be very different from either personal account, reflecting their goals for the relationship rather than their aspirations or limitations as individuals.

But how can you separate relationship karma from the karma of the individuals? I don't see how a relationship can be stronger than either partner, unless you're saying that the relationship itself provides an opportunity for the partners to work out personal issues—and work off individual karma. Using your banking analogy, maybe my partner's responsible approach to money rubs off on me, so I begin to keep my personal account in order. Wouldn't that have a positive effect on the relationship as well?

Very likely. Couples influence one another consciously and unconsciously, and what affects them as individuals has some effect on the relationship and vice versa. One of the great gifts of intimacy is constant feedback. What you say or do seldom escapes your partner's notice, and issues tend to surface. Once you deal with those issues, you can redirect that energy into the relationship. The more attuned to your partner you become, the easier it is to sense trouble ahead and take steps to clear up misunderstandings before they cause harm.

But it seems as if the closer I am to someone, the greater the chances I'll do or say something harmful, however inadvertent. That makes me wonder if it's inevitable that any deep emotional attachment will create negative karma. Could I avoid it by maintaining more emotional distance?

Nearly every relationship produces some troublesome karma. Nobody's perfect, and intimate partners, no matter how much they love one another, are bound to experience friction from time to time. Tinkering with your level of emotional involvement isn't the solution. It would be more fruitful to focus on dealing

" We live in feelings, not in figures on a sundial. We should count time in heartbeats. "

ARISTOTLE (384–322 BCE)

with the inevitable stresses of a relationship. If your tolerance for intimacy is very different from your partner's, how can you satisfy each other's needs regardless? Are you forthcoming about matters like money and family? Are you able to resolve conflict in a respectful way? How do you handle anxiety about fidelity or commitment? Can you tolerate periods of boredom without giving up on each other? Do you interact in a way that's free of manipulation and power plays? All these areas offer a golden opportunity to work out your karma together in a loving way.

What about sex and karma? Is there a connection there?

Consensual sex between adults is one of the great pleasures of human life. It can even generate good karma if it leads to a closer emotional bond or a loved and wanted child. However unusual the practices you engage in, if you agree on them as a couple, and act out of mutual respect and a commitment to cause no harm, there is unlikely to be negative fallout. (Unless, of course, the bracket to which you've fastened the chains pulls the plaster off the wall of your rented flat, and you refuse to reimburse your landlord for the damages ...)

Exploitive sex is another matter. Here, the consequences will be unwholesome for both exploiter and victim. That said, what constitutes "exploitive" is not always clear-cut. If one partner submits only out of a desire to please the other, or from fear of reprisal, it could be argued that the sex is exploitive. However, if the dominant party had no idea that his partner's participation was less than wholehearted—and there was no malicious intent—then it would be harder to call the sex exploitive. We're obliged to take responsibility for our own sexual conduct, and that includes making our needs, wishes, and boundaries perfectly clear.

That raises another question: Is it bad karma to base a relationship solely on physical attraction?

You'd have to see how the relationship played out. Many a relationship has started with physical attraction. It's said that couples link up on the basis of subtle scent signals—each of us has a distinct body odor—but for a lot of people appearance is probably just as compelling. Where you cross the line into negative karmic territory is if one person is in it strictly for the sex—or the ego-boost of being on the arm of someone gorgeous—while the other person is emotionally invested. Unless some sort of parity arises over time, there's bound to be an injured party.

That brings me to a delicate matter: Is there a way to break off a relationship that won't create bad karma?

Again, the key is "Do no harm." Can you sever the ties with mutual respect and sensitivity to how the breakup might affect your partner? Can you divide any property equitably, and settle custody issues in favor of the children's welfare? We can barely exchange phone numbers with someone without creating karma between us. But parting doesn't have to end in years of pain if you keep in mind that the person on the other side of the negotiating table is someone you once vowed to cherish above all others. Even if you're angry enough to strangle your about-to-be-ex, try to remember that hatred only breeds hatred—and binds us to the hated object. Emotionally and karmically, making peace is the wiser course.

Peacemaking Meditation

To dissolve anger toward another person, particularly an intimate partner, try this variation on a classic Tibetan Buddhist teaching: Remember (or imagine) that over the course of infinite lifetimes, your partner has been in every conceivable relationship with you—mother, father, brother, sister, aunt, uncle, daughter, son, and grandparent, as well as lover. You can't help but feel at least a little tenderness.

Dialogue **8**

LIVING
TRUTHFULLY

How to be forthright with sensitivity and skill

Honesty is the glue that binds civilized society together. "Never lie," we're taught as kids. Later on, we discover that truth is not so simple: at times full disclosure may not be the wise or kind response. So how do we discern what makes for an honest life?

Is truth-telling the sine qua non of good karma? I grew up believing it's a sin to lie. But I can think of situations in which telling the truth—the whole truth, anyway—could be harmful. It could hurt someone's feelings, or ruin a reputation, or worse.

Honesty is the core of an ethical life in just about every tradition. Ancient Hindu texts tell us liars go straight to "Raurava hell"—a horrific fate. The *Taittiriya Upanishad* advises,

"LET YOUR CONDUCT BE MARKED BY TRUTHFULNESS IN WORD, DEED, AND THOUGHT."

Saint Augustine—a master prevaricator before he saw the light—declared all lies a sin, whatever the reason. The Buddha held that even a justifiable lie creates negative karma. How negative is a matter of degree. A "white lie" to beg off a dinner invitation would hardly be as injurious as misrepresenting the condition of your car to a prospective buyer or carrying on an extramarital affair.

Dishonesty with intent to harm is always a no-no, but most of our day-to-day falsifying is more venial or less clear cut. We routinely spin half-truths in business and deceive children "for their own good." In the end, however, honesty is more than a calculus of truth and lies. It's an attitude, a posture toward life— a decision to stand by our words and deeds. Honesty begins with self-honesty. Aware, we can respond in good faith to whatever arises.

Sometimes it's hard to know whether to tell the truth or dissemble. Just remember what Mark Twain said:

"WHEN IN DOUBT, TELL THE TRUTH ... IF YOU TELL THE TRUTH YOU DON'T HAVE TO REMEMBER ANYTHING."

But isn't the idea of total honesty a bit quaint? These days everyone—our government included—shades the truth. It's hard to convince anybody that honesty matters.

It's too bad we can't look to our leaders for ethical guidance—even the clergy aren't always moral exemplars. At least we have individuals like Nelson Mandela, Sister Helen Prejean, and the Dalai Lama to demonstrate what it means to live with integrity. A principled life takes work, no question. But when we're tempted to fudge, we should look a little closer and see if a lie is really justified. Often we can find a straight-up approach. Our lives almost never call for the kind of world-class obfuscation that government and industry hide behind. Whenever we resort to duplicity it's usually because we're too lazy to look for an alternative, or we're trying not to hurt someone's feelings.

Like faking an orgasm, you mean? I want to be considerate, but isn't it wrong if I do it too often?

Once in a while is love. Too often, and you've got a problem that's bigger than sex. Find a way to discuss it frankly, if you want your relationship to thrive.

What about feigning interest in what someone is saying?

Some people are just plain boring, and it's hard to engage with them in a truthful way. But instead of going on automatic, why not take the opportunity to practice empathic listening? Don't let your mind wander. If the words are boring, listen for the emotion behind them. You'll start to pick up the subtext of conversations, the true meaning. At that level, nearly everyone is riveting.

What about other forms of pretense? For example, if my mother-in-law gives me a present I don't like, I'm conflicted. Should I pretend to like it? Shall I tell her it's not my taste, or quietly exchange it? And what if my husband gives me an expensive gift that doesn't suit me? Should I be truthful?

Is it really worth antagonizing your mother-in-law over a sweater? Grin and wear it, then stash it in a drawer till the next time she comes over. If your husband consistently gives you expensive presents you don't like, remember that he only wants to please you. Why not thank him profusely, then suggest that in future you go together to pick something out? Often the issue isn't whether or not we should be honest but how we express our feelings. Try to see the situation from the other person's perspective before you open your mouth.

Doesn't honesty mean different things to different people? My sister and her fiancé have reached a stalemate over how much they should

*reveal about their pasts. She believes in total candor, while he
believes in telling on a "need-to-know" basis.*

That's a classic clash of belief systems. To an
absolutist like your sister, withholding the truth is the
same as lying, and nothing can justify it. Her fiancé
takes a more utilitarian view—as long as there's no
intent to deceive, why bother speaking up unless it's
relevant now? My question would be:

IS YOUR SISTER JUST STANDING
ON PRINCIPLE, OR DOES SHE
REALLY WANT TO KNOW EVERY
DETAIL OF HER FIANCÉ'S PAST?

*Her fear is that any secrets will come back to haunt them. What if
there's something in his past that he's ashamed to reveal? Could it
happen again? If he can't be totally open with her, how will they
ever establish a bond of trust?*

There's no question that what we won't talk about

> **" It is not the oath that makes us believe the man, but the man the oath. "**
>
> AESCHYLUS (525–456 BCE)

can assume undue importance. The more we suppress it, the more insistent it becomes. Confession is the traditional way to unburden ourselves: we tell all, we're forgiven, and we put the matter behind us. Or so we hope. But truth delivered out of context, or too soon in a relationship, can result in misunderstanding. The argument against full disclosure has some merit. Maybe your sister's fiancé isn't harboring any shameful secrets after all, but simply wants to maintain some privacy.

As to whether or not total honesty is essential for lasting love, even marriage counselors are divided on this. Most agree at present that partners should be transparent about their lives. But the issue of how much to reveal about the past is something every couple must work out for themselves. The standoff between your sister and her fiancé may be a blessing in disguise, because it will force them to examine their fears and values. Their relationship can only benefit as a result.

Speaking of relationships, the other night I saw a friend's husband dining with another woman. Should I tell her?

This is the question Randy Cohen, the ethics columnist for *The New York Times Magazine*, says he is asked most often. Everyone seems to have a different view. But most agree that before you do anything, you should be sure of the facts. Maybe the husband was entertaining a business associate or an old college chum. The majority opinion is that you should tell your friend only if you're *absolutely sure* she'd want to know. Some couples have a tacit agreement to play around as long as they're discreet, and they wouldn't welcome having their cover blown. If you *do* decide to say something, proceed with caution—and be available if your friend needs a shoulder to cry on.

Are there times when we're morally obligated to speak up about dishonesty? What if someone is spreading malicious gossip, for example?

Gossip and rumors are high on the bad-karma list. If you don't stop their spread, you're complicit. Unmasking other forms of dishonesty is more complex. Is the behavior harmful? Would exposing it cause even greater harm? What's your relationship to the parties involved? It's always tempting to blow the whistle when people do things like park illegally in the disabled slot, or call in sick so they can play a round of golf. But why get involved? Remember that we all have our own karma. True, other people's dishonesty can be galling. Lies not only break the trust between liar and lied-to, they also tear at the fabric of trust underlying society, as the ethicist Sissela Bok has pointed out.

If that's the case then how can even a little white lie have any redeeming value?

Telling your hostess she looks divine may or may not be true but it's kind. She doesn't really want to know that you think she should never, ever wear that shade of blue. You can sidestep an outright lie with a vague comment like "What a color!" or "How chic you look!" In your heart you'll know the truth.

Some people are incapable of telling even social

lies. They stake their reputation on saying exactly what they think, no matter whose feelings are hurt in the process. But candor without wisdom or compassion diminishes both sender and receiver. Kindness, on the other hand, bathes everyone in a positive light. Even the Talmud endorses the well-intentioned fib:

> "YOU MAY MODIFY A
> STATEMENT IN THE
> INTERESTS OF PEACE."

Would that include keeping up a pretense for someone who won't admit she's seriously ill? I want to say, "Face reality before it's too late," but I guess it's not up to me to shatter her illusions.

You don't have to feed someone's illusions *or* take them away. Just be a loving presence, open and accepting. Your steadfastness will be truer than anything words could convey.

OPENING HAND AND HEART

How to show you really care

Generosity is one of humanity's greatest virtues. Offering time, money, love, or a helping hand signals concern for our mutual welfare. Don't agonize over what, when, or how much to give. Don't wait to be asked. Just do it. Giving is a direct path to good karma.

Everywhere I look, I see people in need. I want to help, but the task seems overwhelming. What difference can a few dollars make? With all the worthy causes there are, I get so confused about where and how much to give that I often end up giving nothing at all. Is there a solution?

If we only considered the enormity of the world's problems compared to the paltry amount we're prepared to give, almost everyone would be frozen in inaction. Even the very rich have the same concerns as you: *How much can I afford to give? Where will my contribution do the most good?* Philanthropy is very big business these days, and there are individuals and organizations whose job is to help donors decide where to allocate their contributions in order to make them count. The other half of the equation is determining how much you can realistically afford to give—what percentage of your net worth you can realistically allocate to charitable causes, without causing hardship to yourself and your dependants. Your financial advisor can help you calculate this, or you can consult one of the many websites that offer formulas for giving. But as important as these nuts and bolts considerations are, they touch on only one aspect of generosity. There are a thousand non-material ways to give of yourself. Just serving a meal to others is a bountiful act. Generosity is a major tenet of all the world's religions. When practiced with awareness, it's of as much benefit to the donor as to the recipient.

But isn't giving supposed to involve self-sacrifice—putting others' needs before our own?

We shouldn't give to the detriment of our own welfare, but most spiritual traditions hold that generosity involves at least some self-sacrifice. It's the best antidote to greed. Giving only what you don't want—and only when asked—is the lowest form of generosity, according to Buddhist teachings. The

" Others are my main concern. When I notice something of mine, I steal it and give it to others. "

SHANTIDEVA (8TH CENTURY)

highest form, "kingly" or "queenly" giving, involves giving the very best of what you have—what you would want for yourself. In societies where Buddhist monks subsist on donations—*dana*—for their meals, even the poorest families give generously of their meager supply, reserving the best food for the monks. They believe that in doing this they are "making merit"—that their sacrifices will be rewarded with good karma.

Self-sacrifice doesn't come naturally to everyone, however. We may be generous with our friends and families but balk when it comes to opening our checkbooks or committing our time for a worthy cause. It's hard to imagine most of us following the old admonition to "give till it hurts." Though a small minority use some calculus akin to tithing and give away ten percent or more of their net income, Americans in general allocate less than four percent to charity, and donations earmarked for the poor have dropped precipitously. The 12th-century physician and scholar Rabbi Moses ben Maimon, known as Maimonides, recognized our reluctance when he devised his eight-step Ladder of Charity:

on the lowest rung we give grudgingly, while on the highest we help the needy become self-reliant.

If we tend to give with reservations, I guess we don't really see giving as mutually beneficial.

It depends. When generosity is understood as a gift to God, it is welcomed as a chance to express gratitude by offering up your time, knowledge, skill, money, or possessions. Charity is one of the Five Pillars of Islam, a way of purifying your soul and getting closer to Allah, as well as fulfilling your societal obligation to care for the less fortunate. Ideally, we don't give primarily with an eye to returns, but the generous nearly always reap a reward of some kind, if only the satisfaction of knowing they've helped others.

Doesn't being forced to give—or give a prescribed amount— undermine the spirit of generosity? Isn't that like trying to "buy" good karma? Wouldn't it have a negative effect?

Giving on request or demand may not carry the full karmic benefits of giving voluntarily, but there is still some benefit for both donor and recipient. Don't forget that generosity tends to grow on the giver. Giving makes us feel good, which inspires us to give more. We should never turn down an opportunity to give: we never know where it will lead us or what may happen as a result.

You're not just talking about giving money, I presume.

Not every situation calls for money. We give whatever we have that is appropriate to the occasion and the recipient. Think of the huge outpourings in the wake of recent natural disasters. When officials failed to respond adequately, private citizens stepped in to help, person to person.

Generosity is one of mankind's nobler instincts. When we can see ourselves reflected in others, we're moved to take action.

Is it bad karma to give in exchange for something—a tax deduction, say, or a building with your name on it?

There's nothing wrong with taking a tax deduction for what you give. That's one of the realities of life today, and we can always hope it's not your only motivation. On the other hand, putting your name to a gift diminishes it somewhat in the eyes of some spiritual traditions. For Maimonides, giving anonymously to someone you don't know is the next to highest rung on the Ladder of Charity.

What about giving in someone else's name? Would that produce positive karma?

Very likely. A gift in someone's name—a parent's perhaps—is a wonderful tribute. Instead of making a donation to your alma mater's general fund, with even a modest amount of money you could endow a grant or prize in the person's honor. Every year three scholarship students at a Western New York dental school receive a stipend for books and living expenses donated by a dentist who mentors them in honor of his late father, a graduate of the school.

Is there a way of giving that leads to negative karma? I'm thinking of people whose generosity is self-serving in some way.

There are people whose giving reflects primarily their own needs. They may try to buy others' love with their generosity, but not surprisingly the recipients often feel manipulated instead. Some people give too much, arousing feelings of obligation rather than gratitude: an example is the all-sacrificing mother. Then there are narcissists who give what they think you should have rather than what you need or want. These are the dinner guests who barge into your

" True charity occurs only when there are no notions of giving, giver, or gift. "

THE BUDDHA (C.563–C.483 BCE)

doing the dishes, even when
do them yourself later on.
bring negative karma to the
recipient of the good karma
arefully tendered gift.

RYONE'S BENEFIT
E GIVING WITH
AN OPEN HAND, AN OPEN
HEART, AND NO EXPECTATION
OF RETURN.

APPRECIATING
LIFE'S GIFTS

How to make the most of your experiences

Receiving is giving's partner, and an art in itself. We learn to appreciate what comes to us, whether it's nature's bounty or earthly goods and pleasures, without taking what's not ours or grabbing more than our share. Greed breeds bad karma. Trust tells us there's enough to go around.

Recently one of my colleagues got in trouble for charging her
vacation to her corporate credit card. I would never cheat our
company like that, I told another co-worker. He said I was being
hypocritical. "Don't you ever take home office supplies, or make a
personal long-distance call at work?" he asked. Sure, I said.
Doesn't everybody? It wouldn't occur to me to call that stealing. I
figure it's the least the company owes me, considering the long hours
I put in. Am I off base?

Sounds like you're of a mind with Ralph Waldo
Emerson:

"ALL STEALING IS COMPARATIVE.
IF YOU COME TO ABSOLUTES,
PRAY WHO DOES NOT STEAL?"

Who, indeed? Taking office supplies for use at home
is commonplace. There's even research showing that
morale is higher in workplaces that tolerate a degree
of petty theft. Most of us can justify pocketing the
odd notepad or pen, or making the odd phone call

on our employer's dime. But would you think it right to run up hundreds of dollars in personal phone charges, as some employees routinely do, or to empty the office supply cupboard into your child's backpack, like some parents I know? Probably not.

What about using work time to shop online or take care of other personal matters?

Strictly speaking, that, too, is a form of theft. You're stealing time from your employer. But if you're not flagrantly abusing the privilege, who's likely to stop you? It's up to you to decide what you can live with. If, every time you sign a check, you think, "This pen came from my office," then you've overstepped your own line. At issue is how trustworthy you are. If you feel as if you're putting one over on your boss, you'll never be entirely comfortable at work, and that's bound to affect your performance. One easy way to look at it is: whatever isn't freely given to you isn't really yours.

But what if something's freely given to me, but the giver didn't realize he shouldn't have given it? Say the ticket seller at the movies offers me the senior citizen discount, but I'm too young to be eligible for it. Must I point this out? Movies are so overpriced today. Why shouldn't we consumers get a break?

If the ticket seller gave you too much change, you'd return it, wouldn't you? Similarly, don't accept a discount or any other offer you're not entitled to. Just because we think the cost of living is too high doesn't mean it's OK to play Robin Hood and appropriate whatever goods and services we can get away with. Lots of people who find the cost of movies too high wait and rent the DVD, or choose another form of entertainment. If enough people were to boycott expensive movies, maybe collectively you could bring the price down. But until then, you might ask yourself why you need to act dishonestly just to save a couple of bucks. Is there an element of thrill-seeking here—instead of rappelling down a cliff you try to sneak into the movies? Or is there a larger issue—a sense of entitlement perhaps?

Somehow we've gotten the idea it's our right to have life just the way we want it. In a store the other day I watched a young mother hold up the entire checkout queue while she dickered with her three small sons over what each could or couldn't buy, how much it cost, and who would pay for it. When she

> ## " Remember that what you have now was once among the things you only hoped for. "
>
> EPICURUS (C.341–270 BCE)

finally finished, did she apologize? Not at all. She shot a steely look at us and announced, "My sons and I are *entitled* to shop."

Ouch. I guess I've been acting that way: doing and taking what I want when I want it—and defying anyone to stop me.

It's with good reason that every religion considers greed "the Mother of All Sins," as the writer Phyllis Tickle puts it. "Covetousness alone is a great destroyer of merit and goodness," the yogi Bhishma says in the classic Hindu epic the *Mahabharata*. When we're in the grip of our desires, we're blind to everything and everyone around us. We lose all perspective. Otherwise reasonable, upstanding people pinch silverware and china from their restaurant tables, and help themselves to anything not nailed down in their hotel rooms. Some hotels have even started offering the furnishings for sale in an effort to cut their losses. It isn't need that's prompting this sort of behavior, it's greed.

What's the antidote?

Learning to receive is one solution. We're better at taking what we think we deserve than receiving what life freely offers. All too often we gobble up things and experiences without noticing or appreciating them. It's like being served a delicious, beautifully presented meal and wolfing it down, instead of savoring each dish.

Are you suggesting that we slow down and pay attention?

Exactly. The happiest people are those who draw the most from life, whatever their experiences. Train yourself to be aware of simple things: chatting with a friend, gazing at the moon, walking your dog.

Taking, like stealing, is a one-way transaction: one person's gain is another's loss. Receiving is just the opposite—it's half of a two-way transaction, with giving as its equal partner. Giving and receiving are bound together in a mutually life-enhancing exchange.

Dialogue **11**

HAVING
ENOUGH

How to live well and spend right

"Having it all" is a state of mind. When we're not busy striving to amass money and things, it's amazing how rich our lives can be. True wealth consists in knowing what you need, using wisely what you have, and investing your resources where they'll do the most good.

I know that money isn't everything and that most of us in developed countries overconsume, but whenever I hear about "voluntary simplicity" it sounds so grim and self-depriving. There's even a website that suggests, "You might want to ask if you can survive without a fridge." Can't we live comfortably but responsibly in today's world without having to act like we're back in the 1800s?

Simplicity advocates sometimes forget that life in the past wasn't always idyllic. In the 1800s people may have relied on fresh food rather than refrigeration, but the coal fires they heated their houses with caused terrible air pollution, never mind horrific working conditions for the coal miners. The basic principles of the voluntary simplicity movement—consume less; live within your means; don't waste human and environmental resources—are worthy ideals of an ethical life. But at its most extreme, voluntary simplicity is a lifestyle choice most people aren't prepared to make. We're creatures of the 21st century, faced with certain realities. We can modify our behavior but not change everything overnight.

In my community the realities seem to be earning as much money as possible, living in a big house, and driving an SUV. I may not be ready to trade down to a grass hut and a bicycle, but I can see that a lavish lifestyle isn't sustainable.

No question, the rich are richer these days, and there are more of them. And a lot of that extra money is being spent on luxuries that are using up the world's natural resources at a ferocious rate. Scientists have finally agreed that global warming has us on a disastrous course and that the gas-guzzling, waste-producing lifestyle of the world's wealthier nations is largely to blame. Our collective attitude of entitlement is fueling negative karma. That doesn't mean we're helpless as individuals, however. While we pressure government and industry to play key roles in reversing this downward spiral, we can each do our part by rethinking how we live—what we earn, how we spend, what we save, how we conserve our own and the world's resources.

THERE'S A DISPARITY BETWEEN WHAT WE SAY WE VALUE AND WHAT WE ACTUALLY DO.

But it's hard to keep up in the world today. No matter how much money I make, it never seems to go far enough. How can I make my dollars count?

> That's the big question for a lot of people. It shows you're thinking beyond amassing money for its own sake or to keep up with the neighbors. We all have to meet basic needs for housing, food, clothing, medical care, and the like. There's negative karma in failing to provide for yourself and your dependants. But once those basic needs are met, do we move into the area of wants, or is there another, subtler layer of needs? It's one thing to say human beings have a need for community and a spiritual life—mercifully, there's no price tag on these. But is taking a vacation a need or a want? Is buying a car when you could take the bus? And at what point does a sweater become a luxury, not just body covering?

Now I'm starting to feel guilty, as if buying a cashmere sweater is a sin. Would it be more appropriate, karmically speaking, to buy the cheapest item I can find?

> Not necessarily. Price is only one aspect to consider. You'd have to compare the real costs—human and environmental, as well as financial—of your cashmere

> **If you live according to the dictates of nature, you will never be poor; if according to the notions of humankind, you will never be rich.**
>
> SENECA (4 BCE–65 CE)

sweater and its inexpensive, probably synthetic, counterpart. What resources were used in making the yarn? Did any animals suffer? What wastes did the manufacturing process produce? Was the sweater assembled in a sweatshop, with cheap human labor? By what route did the sweater reach the store? How much warmth does the sweater offer? How much pleasure? The list goes on, but you get an idea of all the steps we need to consider in assessing the real cost of what we buy. Unwittingly we may be contributing to the exploitation of workers, or even, as in the case with so-called "blood" diamonds in Africa, to financing war.

I see your point, but if I submitted every purchase I made to that process—every head of lettuce or tin of coffee—it would take all day.

If we had to deconstruct every purchase, we'd probably think twice about buying so much. In some parts of the world, procuring the basics—food, water, firewood—does indeed take most of the day. Mercifully, we don't have to do that here. But to make sure we're using our buying power to live ethically and responsibly, we need to remain aware of what and why we're buying and, insofar as possible, buy only from stores and manufacturers whose practices don't exploit people or the environment. Conscious consuming can be very liberating on many levels. You buy less and settle for less. Quality becomes more important than quantity or following fads. And when you buy less, you spend less, which means you don't have to earn as much. Your dollars go farther, and you have money left to invest in what's most important to you.

Do you mean supporting causes I care about, or putting money aside for the future, or paying off my debts?

Supporting other people's well-being and securing your own future are both good karmic investments.

As for repaying debts, it's one of the most essential commitments you can make. From a karmic standpoint, it's better not to incur debt—at least not unsecured debt. We know what happens if people lose a job or get sick and can't make their loan payments, or get in over their heads in credit card debt. If you do incur any debt, pay it off as soon as possible, the Buddha said. That is practical wisdom for avoiding bad karma.

Would debt lead to negative karma even it was for something special like a wedding, or a trip, or a new sound system?

A truly sustainable life would not have more money going out than coming in, and extra assets would be invested or kept in reserve. "Don't dip into capital" used to be the mantra of the moneyed classes. Only

❝ Who is rich?
He who rejoices in
his portion. ❞

THE TALMUD

$49.00

the super rich have that luxury today. For most of us there are pressing reasons—education, healthcare— why we need to draw on reserves. If you're going to incur debt or take money from savings, just be honest with yourself about why you're doing it. Whether we're talking about the world's resources or our own, failing to take the future into account as we spend could mean hardship later on. If you can, spend on experiences, not things. There will be less social and environmental impact, and your memories will make you happier than any object.

Do material possessions always lead to bad karma?

It's not things but our desire for them that causes trouble—makes us obsessive, competitive, and prone to reckless choices. Religions recognize this in their teachings on greed. "The love of money is the root of all evil," the New Testament tells us, while the Koran points out that "the mutual rivalry for piling up (the good things of this world) diverts you (from more serious things)"—in other words, God. Seek wisdom, not riches, the Mormons say, and God's mysteries will be revealed. True wealth isn't material, it's spiritual fulfillment.

EARNING RESPONSIBLY

How to work with integrity

Good work is more than just a means to earn a living. It celebrates our creativity and skills, and expresses our values in the marketplace. The best businesses don't serve the bottom line alone but also promote the welfare of people and the planet. Good work creates good karma.

I like my job and the pay is decent, but I have reservations about my company's products—processed foods. We're not doing anything illegal, but we're not selling health food either. Is it bad karma to collect a paycheck from a business I don't entirely approve of?

If your company isn't engaged in any nefarious activities—dumping toxic waste, making fraudulent claims—and you're doing the job you were hired for, you have every right to collect a paycheck. No karmic backlash there. But implicit in your question is a larger issue: Is the company ethical? Is it violating public trust in some way—and, by extension, are you? Ethical companies are concerned with their impact on their employees, customers, shareholders, and the environment, but no business is perfect. No matter how scrupulous its policies and practices, your company has to interface with a less-than-perfect world. Even if it were turning out 100%-organic food, odds are it would be reliant on conventional means of transport to distribute the finished product. We have to be reasonable in setting our standards.

But isn't it hypocritical to sell a product I won't use myself?

If you have an aversion to what your company sells— nothing but fresh foods are welcome on *your* family table—then you might not be comfortable working there in the long run. If you wish, start looking for a workplace more consonant with your values, but there's no need to quit in a karmic huff.

Surely there are jobs that constitute "right livelihood" and those that are just plain wrong from a karmic standpoint?

The Buddha defined right livelihood in terms of what we *shouldn't* do: wrong livelihood is that which involves "scheming, persuading, hinting, belittling, and pursuing gain with gain." He also enjoined us not to engage in business in weapons, human beings, meat, intoxicants, or poison. Most of us would rank arms dealer, contract killer, human trafficker, and sex slave high on any list of bad-karma jobs. But what about the vast array of perfectly legal occupations that broadly fall within the Buddha's parameters—nuclear physicist, publicist, butcher, and bartender, to name but a few?

We can't simply dismiss such jobs as wrong livelihood—the karmic implications will vary widely from case to case. To people who oppose killing of any sort, "exterminator" would be a bad-karma job, yet to residents of mosquito-ridden areas, insecticides are nothing short of lifesaving. Even the most avowedly commercial ventures may sponsor social programs. Ideally we would be able to identify good-karma occupations with certainty. But in reality even the obvious ones—teacher, preacher, healer—if done carelessly, could cause harm.

Then how can I possibly determine which job to take?

After eliminating the obvious—tobacco companies, say, and businesses that exploit natural resources— you could check the social and environmental records of companies and organizations that interest you. Search "socially responsible business" on the Internet, and you'll find websites that identify ethical workplaces and job openings. In right livelihood, as in everything to do with karma, the bottom line is "do no harm." Research the possibilities but let common sense, conscience, and your heart be your guides.

IF A JOB FEELS WRONG, IT *IS* WRONG—FOR YOU, AT LEAST. IF IT FEELS RIGHT, PURSUE IT.

*What's the karmic effect if the only job you can find, or you're
qualified to do, is one with negative associations—say,
telephone sales?*

Sometimes we have to make compromises to make a
living. We can do our best to find work that doesn't
go against our values, but if we can't meet our highest
standards, we should take what's available and do it
with grace. If we act in good faith with others' welfare
in mind, we can reduce the potential for unfavorable
karma. And just for the record, there actually are
people who *welcome* telephone solicitations.

*Recently I read an article in which a prison official talked about
how upset he gets whenever he has to witness an execution. I don't
see why he doesn't just quit.*

If I remember correctly, that prison was the main
source of jobs for miles around. But even in an
extreme situation like that, all is not lost from a
karmic standpoint. In the end it matters less what
we do than how we do it.

Any job can be an opportunity to do good. The
prison official could use his position to create better
conditions in his facility. If he feels strongly enough,
he could even lobby against capital punishment. All

over the country, there are innovative wardens working for prison reform, taking steps to relieve overcrowding and increase inmates' access to education, job training, and spiritual support. Guards, too, benefit from many of the reforms. Some who've been assigned to supervise prison meditation classes say that after seeing how much they helped the inmates, they started meditating, too.

So just about any occupation can foster good karma?

I'm always moved by people who do society's dirty work—collecting trash, cleaning septic tanks, mopping floors—with diligence and good cheer. You can't help but think they're earning good karma by making life easier for everyone around them.

> ❝ Far and away the best prize that life offers is the chance to work hard at work worth doing. ❞
>
> THEODORE ROOSEVELT (1858–1919)

STAYING
HEALTHY

How to feel good and keep your karma clean

The body is a karmic storehouse. Where we've been, what we've done, who our parents are, is coded in our cells. But don't blame karma alone for your ills. Together, diet, fitness, genes, attitude, environment, and other factors hurt or heal us. We can act now for a healthier future.

The other day we took a friend who has cancer to lunch, to cheer her up and let her know we're supporting her in her recovery. Midway through lunch one of the women suddenly turned to our friend and said, "Why do you think you needed to get cancer? What karma are you trying to work out?" Everyone was dumbstruck. It was so cruel. Yet I couldn't help wondering to what extent we might cause our health problems, or what karma might have to do with sickness and healing.

We do a great disservice to people wrestling with serious illness if we suggest that they "caused" their ailment or that it's karmic retribution for past wrongdoing. If you engage in "blaming the victim," it's *your* karma that's likely to suffer. I'm not saying that habits and lifestyle don't influence health and well-being. But it's widely agreed that illness is way too complex to attribute to a single cause. As Buddhist teacher Sharon Salzberg has pointed out, many causes and conditions—near and remote, and often unknowable—give rise to a particular disorder in a particular person at a particular time. The Buddha even said it would be fruitless to try and predict exactly how future karma would play out. So when a friend is sick, don't ask what she did to cause her disease, ask how you can help. If there's to be any discussion of why this is happening, let the ailing person take the lead.

YOU'RE NOT THE KARMA POLICE.

Point taken. But we do hear a lot about the mind's effect on physical health.

And much of it's true. Our state of health is not totally under our conscious control, but we do know, for example, that stress suppresses the immune system, making us more vulnerable to viruses and infections. So we can reduce our chances of illness—and negative karma—by not doing what wears down our resistance. At the same time, we can take preventative actions that are likely to ensure better health. Researchers have found, for example, that mindfulness meditation practiced regularly not only improves the ability to handle the emotional side of stress but also enhances immune function. The subjects of the study, employees of a biotech company, followed an eight-week program that included an hour of meditation a day, six days a week, and an intensive one-day retreat.

I'm still not clear where karma fits into the health equation.

The body is a karmic storehouse. Your genes carry your family health karma. Add to that your conditioning—what you've done with your body—and you have the karmic matrix in which illness and health arise. Just as doctors use your medical history to help make a diagnosis, your karmic history points toward what can help you heal. Often people see illness as a wake-up call—a message from the body not only to take better care of themselves but also to uncover aspects of their inner life that they've been neglecting.

A health crisis can be transforming. "Heal" comes from the Old English word *haelan*, meaning "to become whole." This suggests that healing is a spiritual, as well as physical matter. The process of restoring mind-body balance nearly always involves working off negative karma—changing self-defeating thinking, as well as unwholesome habits. Research shows, for example, that forgiving people we believe have harmed us hastens physical and emotional recovery.

How does diet influence karma? For example, is a vegetarian diet essential for cultivating good karma?

Some people become vegetarian for health reasons—there's a lot of research showing that the high-fat, high-protein Western diet increases our chances of heart disease. Other people adopt a vegetarian diet or a vegan (no animal products) way of life as an ethical stance, often citing the inhumane ways in which most food animals are raised and slaughtered. Given the connection between diet and non-harming, choosing vegetarianism is a way to not only avoid negative karma but also cultivate positive karma, since it is a clear demonstration of compassion for all living creatures.

Is the converse also true—eating meat will add negative karma to my plate?

It could, if you believe that killing animals is wrong. But even though Buddhist doctrine, for one, prohibits killing animals, some Buddhists include meat or fish in their diets. How do the devout reconcile this? Intention. If you kill animals only for sustenance and

> **" He who has health,
> has hope. And he who has hope,
> has everything. "**
>
> ARABIAN PROVERB

do it consciously and humanely, negative karma will accrue—but not nearly as much as if you act without thinking.

So once again, motivation is all when it comes to karma?

Intention is one of the most significant factors in determining whether or not some contemplated action is likely to produce bad karma.

IT PAYS TO THINK AHEAD.

What about dietary self-indulgence? Should I avoid treats like expensive chocolates in order to stay karmically pure?

Dark chocolate, at least, has been found to be good for us, so you can rationalize it as health food. But your question seems to be coming from a more puritanical place: Is it ever all right to eat for pleasure? I can only say, "Go for it." Food is one of the few treats that usually doesn't have negative consequences. Just avoid overeating—and high-risk delicacies like raw blowfish.

Speaking of risks, I've been arguing with friends about whether recreational drug use creates bad karma or is neutral, as long as you're not abusing drugs or selling them or giving them to minors.

Drug use is commonplace, but that doesn't make it harmless. At best it's irresponsible—a karmic no-no, especially if you have dependants. Drug *abuse* is an even greater threat to your health and your karma. Buddhist ethics forbids intoxicants on the premise that a clear head makes more considered—and considerate—choices. And don't forget that almost no recreational drug except alcohol is legal. So why put a blot on your karmic rap sheet?

My friends suggest there's something unethical about another common practice—cosmetic surgery. Elective surgery drives up the cost of health insurance premiums, they argue, so we end up paying for somebody else's tummy tuck. But please tell me that a nose job or breast augmentation or the odd Botox shot isn't going to leave me working off karma for the rest of my life?

It probably comes down to the question, what are you doing the cosmetic procedure for? Presuming you're not trying to create a new identity to escape the law, is your motivation simply to feel better about yourself? Many women who've had nose surgery as teens say it's made a lifelong difference in their self-esteem. Are you trying to look fifteen or twenty years younger so you can stay in the dating or professional game? If so, maybe you need to consider the values you're buying into. Putting appearance above personal integrity and proficiency may leave you with a karmic hangover down the line. Increasingly, women—and some men—are treating themselves like major renovation projects. If your mental health absolutely depends on it, then probably you can live with any karmic fallout. But please don't be like that 29-year-old woman who's been all over the news for her plastic surgery addiction. "Before" pictures show a pretty blonde. Now, some thirty surgeries later, she's grotesque, her features barely identifiable as human, and still she can't wait to schedule the next operation. If you want to cultivate good karma, let it begin with self-respect.

Dialogue **14**

ASSUMING
YOUR PLACE

How to join the crowd and still be yourself

We're not here just to work out individual karma. Our lives are entwined with the karma of our time, our place, our culture. We're born into a family, a community, and a nation. So how does collective karma affect us? What are our obligations to the group?

I know I'm responsible for my own karma. But I'm not living in this world alone. First there's my family. Does what I do affect their karma and what they do affect mine?

Of course. People who live in the same household have years, maybe lifetimes, of collective experience. Though each of you has individual karma, your fortunes are intertwined. But are you forever burdened with the shame and sorrow of your kin? Do their good works reflect well on you, or wipe your karmic blackboard clean? Not necessarily. We're constantly reinventing ourselves and, to the extent we can, working off karma from the past. And let's not forget that our relatives are not our only collective bond. We're also part of a larger clan—the human family—and an ever-shifting array of alliances. Think of all the groups you've ever belonged to—school, work, social circle, neighborhood, community, political party, religion, ethnic group, nation. Each has its own karma.

It sounds like even my book group is karmically linked to me.

Now you're catching on. Ask yourself: If one member of the group couldn't afford to buy the book assigned for the month so she stole a copy from the local bookshop, would the group as a whole bear any responsibilty as a result?

I'd say it's her problem if she doesn't have the money for the book—or doesn't tell the group so we could lend her a copy or even chip in and buy her one.

Now it sounds as if you think the group may have some responsibility after all—morally, at any rate. Could it be that the collective decision to read a particular book obliges the group as a whole to make sure every member has access to it?

Put that way, I suppose I'd agree, though I still wouldn't go so far as to hold the group responsible for an individual's wrong behavior. At most, we could prevent it perhaps. That raises another question: When children act up, whose karma is affected—the kids', the parents', or both?

We're responsible for teaching our children right behavior, yet at the same time we can't prevent them from making their own mistakes. It's what happens after the mistake is made that determines the extent of the karmic consequences.

Let's say my son Johnny and his friend Billy are involved in a playground accident. When I ask Johnny about it, he says it wasn't an accident—he pushed Billy off the jungle gym on purpose. Now

I'm dealing with a child who not only harmed a playmate but also shows no remorse. What can I do?

You face two issues here. You have a behavior problem—an aggressive child who doesn't yet comprehend the difference between right and wrong. And you have a parenting problem—your own guilt and dismay at having failed to teach your child how to play well with others and not hurt anyone. But unless little Billy is lying in the hospital in a coma, nothing that's happened so far is likely to have long-range negative consequences, provided you seize the opportunity to instill in your child the lessons and values he needs to learn. The very act of working with your son on this matter, and guiding him through making amends to his friend, may well produce enough positive karma to offset the initial wrong. And anything you do to strengthen the parent-child bond is a good hedge against future misbehavior.

So maybe collective karma isn't such a bad thing, if it gives me a chance to right a wrong and bond with the people in my world. But what about the broader collective? What is my responsibility to the greater community, for example? How will its karma affect me?

These are critical questions: Where do individual and collective karma intersect? What is our responsibility to the group? Some would say we're responsible for the actions of our elected officials— we chose them, after all—so we share in the karma of their decisions. In reality, most of us aren't in a position to exert much influence, but that doesn't mean we should suffer in silence. In fact, from a karmic standpoint, we have a duty to speak out. Let's say your community board is re-zoning your neighborhood in order to raise property taxes. You're outraged: it's obvious their goal is to drive out middle-class residents and make way for luxury development. You can sit and stew (and rack up negative karma), or you can take action: demonstrate at town hall, lobby your representatives, endorse

" What is hateful to you do not do unto others. That is the entire law. The rest is commentary. **"**

RABBI HILLEL (1ST CENTURY BCE)

sympathetic candidates and legislation—maybe even pray for your leaders. Your responsibility is to follow through on your concern for the problem and for everyone affected.

Remember: Karma follows intention. If your intention is to find a fair and amicable solution, whatever the outcome you won't be tainted with the karma of shortsighted local officials.

What about an event like a plane crash or terrorist attack? Do I bear any responsibility there? Is my karma affected?

Unless you financed the attack or set off the bomb— or are unlucky enough to be one of its victims— you're karmically in the clear. Collective events have proximate causes and distant causes, and the more people involved, the less likely it is that you personally could foresee or forestall it in any way. Even if the chain of causality leads to political or philosophical ideals you share, trying to assign yourself a key role in a large-scale collective event is, generally speaking, a sign of ego. If you want to change the world, focus closer to home.

So ultimately, what collective karma teaches is that we take responsibility for the whole by tending our own tiny patch of it?

Yes, and that means being careful and considerate, even in the most casual exchanges. Those one-off encounters with people you'll never see again—the guy who steps on your foot on the train, the woman whose foot you step on—are a direct experience of collective karma. They show us how lives that barely brush one another in passing can, in a small way, alter our future.

Realizing that we're all connected makes it harder to rationalize selfishness. Say you're caught in a traffic jam, but the restricted bus lane is clear, so you figure, why not? Well, if everybody drove in the bus lane, you'd be right back where you are now—stuck in traffic. Collective karma is about everybody. It lets us know that, like it or not, our behavior affects— and is affected by—everyone around us. As the comedienne Lily Tomlin once quipped:

"WE'RE ALL IN THIS TOGETHER—BY OURSELVES."

THE WHAT-IF-EVERYBODY TEST

How can you make sure your actions will have a positive effect and do no harm? You can submit them to the "What if everybody ...?" test. This is a variation on the universality principle philosopher Immanuel Kant proposed as a way to determine if behavior we're considering is ethically sound. To weigh the karmic implications ask yourself, "What would happen if everybody did this?" or "How would I feel if everybody did this?"

Dialogue **15**

BEING
TOGETHER

How to live in harmony with everything

*Science and spirit agree: we exist in a web of
interrelationship. Humanity is but one strand
in the vast network of animals, plants,
mountains, oceans, and air comprising our
earthly home. Our well-being depends on
courtesy to one another, our survival on
global care. Karma turns on respect.*

Our beloved family cat is old, in failing health. The veterinarian says treatment would be painful and debilitating, and recovery is uncertain. Is it wrong to consider euthanasia? I don't want her to suffer.

Nearly every pet owner faces this question at one time or another. There is no easy answer. Some people vehemently oppose euthanizing pets, arguing that it goes against the natural cycle of life. Others give qualified approval so long as the motive truly is to relieve the pet's suffering and not to avoid the inconvenience or expense of lengthy care. Karmically speaking, the jury is still out. There are countless stories of devoted owners hand-feeding their infirm pets and administering dialysis or other treatments. On the other hand, even though mercy killing produces karma, loving intentions may offset the negative consequences. If you take a pet's life, you might want to consider what Randy Cohen, the ethics columnist for *The New York Times Magazine*, has suggested: Save a life by adopting an animal from a shelter. As you weigh such decisions, bear in mind that animals have their own karma. Sometimes we try to keep a pet alive for selfish reasons when it would be kinder to let it go. Just as you would give hospice care to a dying person, you could make the pet as comfortable as possible without taking measures to prolong its life.

I feel a deep connection with animals, which poses some dilemmas. Recently friends gave me an expensive tin of beluga caviar that I can't bring myself to eat. Wild beluga sturgeon are all but extinct, and the U.S. has banned further imports of the caviar. Everyone says I should enjoy this delicacy while it's still available, but to me, it seems like bad karma to eat the eggs of a fish that's being wiped out by human greed.

Rather than being judgmental about consuming animals for food, we might consider what Zen master John Daido Loori has pointed out: "There is not a single creature on the face of this earth that takes a meal without doing so at the expense of another life." However, your concern for an endangered species is admirable. Since eating the caviar would obviously distress you, why not pass the tin along to somebody without such scruples? You can always take consolation in the good karma you'll earn from standing up for the sturgeon.

It's the human animal that worries me most. Common courtesy seems to have vanished. Take cellphones—nobody can talk on them without disturbing everyone around them. Surely this lack of consideration is bad karma.

It's hard to put a karmic price on technology, but if we could, cellphone use would run high. Bad phone manners aren't a crime, but they brutalize quality of life. What to do about that is another matter. We don't seem to realize how far our voices carry or how oblivious we are when we take calls while driving or walking down the street. One thing you can do is be mindful of your own cellphone use. If we were all as careful as we'd like others to be, a more responsive ethic would emerge. In the meantime, use any creative means you can think of to bring cellphone

❝ When your neighbor's wall is burning, it becomes your business. ❞

HORACE (65–8 BCE)

users to their senses—humor, surprise. And don't underestimate the power of group pressure. On a bus recently a phone user was being so obtrusive that another passenger finally yelled at him to pipe down. The entire bus broke out in applause, and the man slunk off at the next stop. We also need to lobby for more cellphone-free areas and promote those that already exist, such as airplanes and "quiet cars" on trains. As Christine Rosen of the Ethics and Public Policy Center has suggested,

"WE NEED TO APPROACH OUR PERSONAL TECHNOLOGIES WITH A GREATER AWARENESS OF HOW THE PURSUIT OF PERSONAL CONVENIENCE CAN CONTRIBUTE TO COLLECTIVE ILLS."

Cellphone misuse is only one example of what seems to be a widespread lack of awareness. In the city where I live, parents use baby strollers like battering rams to shove their way through crowds. And their kids? They run amok in stores, in restaurants, on public transportation. But if you say anything to the parents, they accuse you of being anti-child.

Counterattack is a common ploy we all use to divert attention from our own behavior. But before you take parents to task, remember that most of them regard any criticism of their children's behavior as a personal insult, as well as an assault on them and their parenting skills. Use diplomacy in such situations. Children are easily distracted, so sometimes all it takes to quiet them is to redirect their attention. Parents are less likely to take offense if your intervention is matter-of-fact and non-judgmental.

Easier said than done. Manners are a lost art nowadays. Sometimes it's hard to have a civil exchange. We demand respect from one another and get mad if we don't get it. What's the answer?

Put simply, we have to realize that, friend or enemy, we're all connected and that civility is our only shot at not destroying one another. The upside to the

> **Civility is not a tactic or a sentiment. It is the determined choice of trust over cynicism, of community over chaos.**
>
> THOMAS JEFFERSON (1743–1826)

current manners crisis is that a new field is emerging—etiquette counseling—and etiquette courses are even cropping up in colleges. Clients for this new brand of coaching include everyone from upwardly mobile executives to children whose parents lack the patience—or know-how—to pass along basic social skills.

Every culture has rules for proper behavior. What's de rigueur might vary from one place to another, but prominent on every list is courtesy. Mystic and author Andrew Harvey notes that the Sufi code of conduct, *adab*, rests on what one scholar described as a "profound courtesy of the heart that arises from a deep relationship with the divine and expresses itself

in refined behavior of all kinds with other beings."
A person with *adab* shows "tenderness toward all
creation," Harvey adds.

*That sounds like a recipe for good karma. But doesn't "tenderness
toward all creation" have a limit? Would it mean, for instance,
that I couldn't bring sand home from the beach for my son's
aquarium because doing so would diminish the environment?*

If everyone who went to the beach brought home
a bucket of sand, the beaches of the world might
indeed be diminished. But the oceans are continually
grinding up shells and stones to create new sand.
Earth replenishes herself so long as we don't interfere
too much. The problem, of course, is that we've
already interfered way too much, defiling the natural
world and exhausting its resources, collectively
accumulating very bad karma as a result.

What's the solution? We can't stop consuming altogether.

It comes back to respect, to a basic regard for one
another and for everything—animal, vegetable, and
mineral—on the planet. When we truly grasp our
interdependence, we find it hard to ignore the fate
of a seagull or a stone or a Dinka tribesman.

Dialogue **16**

HELPING OTHERS

How to heal the world with karma yoga

Karma yoga is selfless service—action reflecting our awareness that we're all in this life together. In a world that at times seems unjust or uncaring, every act of concern spreads hope and goodwill. When we do good works, we not only help others, we help ourselves.

What, exactly, is karma yoga? Is it some sort of exercise or spiritual practice?

You could say that. Based on ancient Hindu teachings, karma yoga is the path of action, as distinguished from the path of contemplation. It doesn't involve just any action but activities directed at what the *Bhagavad-Gita* calls

"THE WELFARE OF THE WORLD."

So it's self-sacrifice, you mean?

Not entirely. In a lot of very practical ways, when we're doing good for others we're also doing good for ourselves. Doing good makes us feel good. And helping to better the lot of people with very little raises the quality of life for us all. That's not the same as saying our motivation is selfish.

Would the kind of thing I see some teens involved in these days be considered good works that are selfishly motivated? They're doing volunteer work but seem to be doing it primarily because it looks good on a college application.

No doubt some teens are exploiting these situations,

but I'll bet most youthful volunteers are sincerely motivated by a sense of doing what's right. Some are even devising very innovative forms of service.

You can't fault young people for wanting to show themselves to advantage—college admission is so competitive. Is burnishing their image any different from what a job seeker does in making sure his CV casts him in a favorable light with potential employers? Good works only become ethically questionable when they're done *solely* for appearances or selfish ends.

If our motivation's pure, can doing good counteract the effects of self-seeking in other areas?

That's the thinking of many spiritual traditions. Vedanta and Buddhism teach that "making merit" is a way of accruing positive karma and working off negative karma, in order to secure a favorable rebirth. Christians believe that good works will earn them a place in heaven. But we don't have to wait for the afterlife or the next life to reap the rewards of caring, or to see the difference doing good can make for ourselves as well as for others. Daily life offers limitless opportunities to help. Observant Jews consider charitable activity the highest calling. And what better way for the super rich to invest the enormous fortunes they've amassed in recent years than in supporting health, education, and social welfare?

What about all the businesses involved in good works? Aren't these "do-gooder" efforts just a lot of corporate PR? Isn't self-interest the motivation?

If we only endorsed charitable activities that were 100 percent altruistic, nothing positive would ever get done. Nearly every good deed has some tinge of self-interest. Sure, corporate charity is good publicity and good for the corporate image. But that doesn't mean all corporate do-gooders are as self-serving as you suggest. Look at some of the corporate donors in the aftermath of Hurricane Katrina. They weren't just throwing money at the problem; many were assessing the devastated region's needs and supplying everything from vital goods and equipment to technical expertise—more than what government was doing, in many cases. Some corporate donors responded to the crisis at the urging of their employees, whose grassroots efforts matched—or even exceeded—company contributions. The relief efforts after large-scale disasters demonstrate what motivated individuals and businesses can do.

Are you saying, if you see a need, fill it?

Why not? After Hurricane Katrina school kids in New England were filling book bags with school supplies and sending them to kids down South. Individuals were opening their homes to whole families they'd never met. Neighbors, co-workers, and church groups were boxing up essentials and delivering them to affected areas. People were putting up websites and hotlines to help survivors track family and pets lost in the storm. Celebrities weren't just organizing fundraisers, they were driving truckloads of supplies to distribution points and joining search-and-rescue parties. The media weren't just reporting the story; they were providing critical services to the stranded. Similar things happen after every disaster.

Why do we do all that? Why do we give? Is it guilt?

Altruism is innate in humans and many animals. Even a small act of generosity gives us a sense of being useful. It used to be that extended families and neighbors helped one another as a matter of course.

Now we have to rely on the kindness of strangers.

> SOMETIMES IT'S OUR TURN
> TO BE THE STRANGERS THAT
> OTHERS RELY ON.

What if you try to help, with every good intention, but your efforts go awry? Isn't it better to do nothing than do the wrong thing?

What could possibly go so wrong that it isn't worth at least an honest effort? Rescue workers know they won't be able to save everyone, but that doesn't keep them from doing all they can. And how can you be sure that the results have gone awry? Maybe they're just not what you expected or planned. Maybe you can't foresee a positive outcome down the line.

In trying to help, is there such a thing as being too self–sacrificing?

Well, the martyr comes to mind. Exhausting oneself while doing things for others isn't good karma, it's a form of self-abuse. And we might call it "too self-sacrificing" to dive into roiling waters to save a drowning swimmer, only to end up drowned yourself. I'm not suggesting that we shouldn't help people in trouble. Just that we should know our limits. If you're not a strong swimmer, toss a life ring to the drowning person, or tether yourself to something on shore before you leap to the rescue. Metaphorically speaking, whenever you're prompted to save someone in deep—or hot—water, be sure you have the strength and the right equipment for the job. Otherwise, call for help. You always want to be part of the solution, not the problem.

What about activism in the political arena? Isn't it harder to be sure you're part of the solution, since it often isn't a matter of right and wrong but of differing views? I may think I'm on the side of the angels, but the opposition probably feels the same way. What are the karmic consequences of taking a position on a political issue or candidate?

As you suggest, just because we passionately support a person or position doesn't necessarily mean it's the most ethical or beneficial one. Hitler believed in what he was doing, yet we categorically condemn his policies and regime. In a democratic system we uphold everyone's right to have—and to air—their beliefs, but not to act out those beliefs if they threaten anyone's safety or human rights. We tolerate diversity until somebody starts throwing stones. Then there's karma to pay.

When I want to be of service to my fellow beings, how can I be sure I'm doing the right thing?

If your motivation is sincere and your methods do no harm, then proceed. You won't know the outcome till you've taken the action. In the *Bhagavad-Gita* Lord Krishna tells the warrior Arjuna he must do what is necessary without attachment to the fruits, in this way serving as an example to others. Keep that in mind and you won't go far wrong.

❝❝ When you come upon a path that brings benefit and happiness to all, follow this course as the moon journeys through the stars. ❞❞

THE BUDDHA (c.563–c.483 BCE)

A Karmic Encounter

Karmic opportunities are all around us. One afternoon I stopped for gas at a station on the freeway and was struggling with the pump when a young couple in a sports car pulled in behind me. I asked the driver if he would mind giving me a hand. Before he could answer, the woman next to him piped up, "I'll do it," and leapt out of the car. To my astonishment, she not only showed me how to work the pump but pumped the gas for me. As the tank was filling, we chatted. It seems the couple were en route to New York City for the weekend to celebrate their fifth wedding anniversary. When the tank was full, I thanked the young woman, and fumbling in my purse, produced a $20 bill. "Please have a glass of champagne on me to celebrate," I told her. "Oh, no," she said, waving away the money. "I just believe it's good karma to help people."

Dialogue **17**

BALANCING
THE SCALES

How to play fair and patch up conflicts

Are you tempted to retaliate when others wrong you? Do you seek retribution for every hurt or slight? Revenge only makes matters worse. Look for appropriate ways to achieve justice. Acknowledge your own role in conflicts and be forgiving. And remember: karma has its own ways of restoring balance.

I understand the basic principle of karma—"What goes around, comes around." When I've done something wrong, I usually find out pretty quickly. But what if someone wrongs me—lies to me, say, or cheats me? Wouldn't I be justified in retaliating? After all, the Bible says, "An eye for an eye …"

Revenge is sweet—for about five minutes. Then you realize you're likely to suffer, too. Remember what Gandhi said about retaliation:

"AN EYE FOR AN EYE MAKES THE WHOLE WORLD BLIND."

The Biblical injunction wasn't meant to encourage retaliation but to make sure the punishment didn't exceed the crime. If you take it upon yourself to punish someone or even the score, you'll only make the situation—and your own karma—worse. Karma is an impartial justice keeper: it brings human folly into line without our intervention.

But what if someone owes me money or has taken something from me? Don't I have a right to recover it?

By all means, try to recover your property or collect a debt. But see if you can do it without being self-righteous or losing your temper. When you retaliate, you're less likely to express yourself effectively and therefore less likely to resolve the situation to your satisfaction. Focus on what you want and be firm about asking for it, but don't get into name-calling or accusations. You'll only put the other person on the defensive.

Sometimes the person gets defensive before I've even said anything. I'm thinking of my stockbroker. My portfolio is way down in value this quarter, and I'm pretty annoyed that my broker hasn't managed it better. I really think he should make it up to me

" Forgiveness is the economy of the heart ... it saves the expense of anger, the cost of hatred, the waste of spirits. "

HANNAH MOORE (1745–1833)

somehow—at least apologize and explain what went wrong—but he won't even return my calls.

Investments are a calculated risk, and markets go up and down. Unless your broker has defrauded you in some way, he isn't liable to cover your losses. However, avoiding your calls isn't very responsible. If you've given it sufficient time and you still can't get through to him, write him a letter stating clearly that you need a broker who's accessible and if that's not how he works, you'll move your account elsewhere. Take responsibility, don't plot revenge—you're the one in charge. And if you do decide to switch brokers, be sure to research the alternatives before making a move.

If I feel that someone has taken advantage of me, I can't seem to stop thinking, "I hope he suffers for this," or "I'll get him."

Vengeful thoughts only confuse the issue. Sing, repeat a mantra—do anything it takes to block those thoughts. Once your mind is calmer you can figure out the most productive action to take. Your stockbroker may be avoiding you because he's afraid you're going to be angry or accusing. You'll get better results if you take an exploratory tack: *How did this happen? What's going on with the market? How are recent market fluctuations reflected in the performance of my portfolio? What might prevent further losses?* If you can concentrate on the facts and keep your feelings out of the conversation, you'll be more likely to gather the information you need to settle the matter.

Should the other person's karma be my concern?

Yes and no. Since as individuals we each have our own karma, for the most part we do well to keep the focus on our own intentions and behavior. Let other people learn their own lessons. They don't need us to play karma cop. All this changes, however, when collective behavior is involved. Let's say you're the boss: the people you supervise are your responsibility, at least in regard to what happens on company premises and company time. If you ask them to take illegal or immoral actions, or risk their health or safety on the company's behalf, you're jeopardizing their karma as well as your own. Most of the time, we don't sit around thinking, "Oh, I shouldn't do this because it will affect so-and-so's karma." But we owe it to others to act with integrity and empathy.

In that sense you *are* your brother's keeper.

But I'm still confused about how to respond when people do something wrong—especially if I'm on the receiving end. How can I deal with the situation in a way that's fair to all concerned?

Justice as we know it is retributive. The state metes out a punishment that usually involves separating the wrongdoer from society at large. But there's an emerging field called restorative justice that focuses on bridging the divide between society and wrongdoer. The guilty person apologizes to the victim and makes restitution for harm done. The method isn't perfect, but there are some amazing stories of healing as a result. Making amends to people you've wronged is also central to the Twelve Step recovery program. Even if you feel you're the aggrieved party, drawing up a list of everyone you're having difficulties with is very revealing. People who've harmed us have suffered from *our* behavior, if we've been resentful or withholding or rejecting toward them. Making amends may not bring reconciliation—some damage is too grave—but acknowledging our common humanity opens the door to forgiveness.

WIPING THE SLATE CLEAN

How to create a better future

How do we get rid of negative karma? Do we pray for forgiveness and start afresh? Must we first right our wrongs, resolve inner conflicts, and recast our thinking? Can good deeds cancel out misdeeds and misjudgment? It's time to discover how karma plays itself out and to plan for a better future.

I want to clear up the mistakes of the past and move on, but I'm not sure how to get rid of negative karma. Are there actions I can take, or do I have to wait for divine forgiveness?

This is one point on which the teachings of East and West diverge. Christianity, Judaism, and Islam all embrace the idea of divine intercession—God or Yahweh or Allah has the power to forgive our transgressions and wipe the slate clean. In the East, where teachings on karma originated, we find a different approach. For Buddhists, there's no external force promising deliverance. As the Theravada Buddhist teacher Mahasi Sayadaw explained, "A Buddhist who is fully convinced of the law of karma does not pray to another to be saved but confidently relies on [himself] for his own emancipation." In this view, releasing karma is a process—a by-product of awareness that emerges with time and effort. In place of prayers for grace are practices like meditation and yoga that allow us to "work creatively with our own suffering," as Reginald Ray, a teacher of Tibetan Buddhism, puts it. We develop insight into the workings of the mind and the causal mechanism of karma.

Both Western psychology and Eastern spiritual practices cast light on the emotional reactivity and habitual thinking that lock us into self-defeating ways of acting and produce negative karma. Our job is to identify those patterns so we can stop repeating the harmful behavior.

Is that what "releasing karma" means?

Releasing, clearing, burning, exhausting, trans-forming—these are all ways of describing the process of working through karma we've accumulated. Karma is not something we simply toss away when we tire of it, like an overcoat that's no longer in style. Psychiatrist Paul Fleischman calls karma a "description of our personality—a unique combination of forces, values, beliefs, predispositions, and reactions" that we've either brought with us from previous lifetimes or developed in this one. Just as karma represents a conflux of factors, so too does its ripening and release. We get rid of some karma simply by living— by allowing our habit patterns to play out without judging or resisting them.

> **"BUDDHISM TEACHES US THAT IT IS IMPORTANT TO LET KARMA RIPEN IN AN OPEN AND FEARLESS WAY,"**

explains Reginald Ray. When we can experience our thoughts, feelings, and memories "without comment, reaction, or intervention," he adds, "the karma exhausts itself, the debt it implies is discharged, and positive karma is generated."

Allowing karma to exhaust itself seems easy enough when I'm sitting on my meditation cushion, but what happens in daily life? Are there specific ways to help the process along?

One action you can take is to make up for ways you've upset or inconvenienced others. That might mean repaying a debt, repairing or replacing property you've damaged, returning something you took, or stopping hurtful behavior. We often hear the phrase "righting a wrong." Making a conscious effort to clean up the past and honor your commitments begins the process of restoring balance in your life. Doing good works also burns off karma. Practicing kindness and generosity helps cancel out bad karma arising from self-seeking and greed. According to New Age teachings, karma is stored in the body's energy field. Meditation on sound or light is said to release these karmic memories.

Can we ever wipe the slate clean—get rid of bad karma altogether?
Eastern teachings hold that only an enlightened mind is completely free of karma. For most of us the goal is to release at least some of the psychological blocks and mental habits that keep us prisoners of our emotions and erroneous beliefs.

What we're talking about is inner transformation —a change of perspective. Karma is tied up with our drives and desires, and the misguided ways we act them out. When we can begin to see even our painful experiences in a wider context—as part of our spiritual evolution—our focus shifts from self-pitying attempts to avoid discomfort ("How can I put this tragedy behind me and never suffer again?") to "What lessons can I learn from this situation?"

Seen from this perspective, releasing karma is a natural part of inner development: we learn the lesson and the karma clears.

What's the immediate payoff from clearing karma?

For one thing, your life will be smoother. Think how much of your energy is now tied up in being angry, or self-serving, or depressed—or in worrying about what you've said and done. Then recall how much better you feel when you clear up a disagreement, or help someone in need, or spend a turmoil-free day. Negative karma consumes time and energy we could better devote to positive action.

Sounds like releasing karma is an ongoing task. Where do I start?

By taking an honest look at your life and your way of thinking. Any process that increases self-awareness will help with this—counseling, mindfulness practice, a self-inventory. Once you've developed the habit of self-reflection, you'll be quicker at identifying opportunities to release negative karma, and better able to avoid the traps in behavior and thinking that create bad karma in the first place.

LIVING WITH CONVICTION

How to stick to your principles

When should you speak out? When should you let things be? It takes guts to stand up for what you believe, even if it means going against the crowd. Doing what's right is your duty to yourself and the world. But there's an art to it. Integrity fosters good karma. Let your conscience guide you.

My friend insists it doesn't matter what we do, as long as we're not hurting anyone. I say we never know who might be affected by our actions, so we should always strive to do the right thing. Is one of us being naïve?

> It may seem as if your views are diametrically opposed, but from another perspective you're closer to agreement than you think. You both want to do what's right and appropriate and doesn't cause harm. The difference lies in whose standards you're using to define the right thing. Perhaps *you're* concerned with following the precepts of your religion or the norms of your community, while your friend is relying more on an inner authority—her conscience or intuitive guidance. We all want to make wise choices. For that we need a moral center—one that's strong enough to hold us steady in all situations, yet flexible enough to bend with the winds of change. Living from that center is one of our greatest challenges.

But how can I be sure I'm taking the right action? If I defer to a higher authority, at least I have some sort of guide beyond my own wishful thinking.

> Relying on your own counsel, your own moral center, doesn't mean you have to go it alone. It's always

smart to check out inner guidance with someone you trust. That could be a spiritual counselor, or a therapist, or simply a friend or family member who can listen to you objectively and offer unbiased feedback. One gift of meditation practice is that as you quiet down, you can hear the wisdom of your higher self above the chatter of your ordinary mind.

FOLLOWING YOUR INTUITION DOESN'T MEAN LEAVING REASON AND COMMON SENSE BEHIND. BE SURE OF THE FACTS IN ANY SITUATION BEFORE YOU PUT YOUR INTEGRITY ON THE LINE.

I'd have to be sure of more than the facts before I put my integrity on the line. Let's say I found out that the company I work for was doing something unethical or illegal. If I spoke up about it, I'd *probably be fired, but if I didn't, people would be hurt. Either way, there would be negative karma. Where would my obligation lie?*

No question, it takes great courage to be a whistle-blower. Speaking out might indeed mean losing your job and suffering hardship—at least in the short term. But if you're sure of the evidence, taking action is the greatest service you can do for everyone who might be affected directly or indirectly by the company's wrongdoing now and in the future. Yes, there would be risk involved in exposing the company's malfeasance. But even if, as you fear, you were fired as a result, it's possible you might not suffer as much as you envisioned. The courage it takes to follow your conscience is exactly the strength of character many organizations are looking for. Who knows? You might even decide to work from the outside on corporate reform.

But what if I decided just to stay at the company and keep my mouth shut? It might be frustrating, but there wouldn't be any risk.

Don't bet on it. Not speaking out might carry even graver consequences than whistle-blowing. Think of all the people who would suffer. And don't imagine you could just walk away from your conscience. It's

Action is eloquence ...

WILLIAM SHAKESPEARE (1564–1616)

not likely to let you forget. Failing to do what we know to be right creates negative karma. We can't always predict the outcome of our actions, but when we act in good faith with a genuine desire to help, we're more likely to make a positive contribution. I think there's probably a special place in heaven for people who don't back down when their beliefs and integrity are tested.

What about other instances of standing on principle? Sometimes I'm not sure to what lengths I should go. As an animal rights advocate should I refuse to let people into my home if they're wearing leather or fur? Is it betraying my principles to dine with meat-eaters?

One thing about karma: it doesn't require us to pass judgment on others. Maybe the fur-wearing meat-eaters of your acquaintance will be reborn in the next life as sheep being fattened for slaughter. Meantime, their habits are not your concern. If you're dining together in a restaurant and they're chowing down on steak and lobster, you can either enjoy the company along with your pasta primavera, or politely excuse yourself and leave. Either way, you needn't embarrass or shame others with elaborate explanations. There's nothing to prevent you from slipping in a line or two about the benefits of a meatless diet, or from showering them with PETA [People for the Ethical Treatment of Animals] literature *if they show interest*. Otherwise, just stick to your principles and trust that your good example will eventually carry the message. At the same time, you don't need to let others run roughshod over your cherished beliefs. If you want to post a sign on your front door saying "Leather- and fur-free zone," by all means do so. It might be courteous to warn guests in advance to leave their leathers and furs at home, or, at the very least, to place a shoe rack near the door.

Whatever beliefs you hold, wear them graciously. Even the best intentions will backfire if you make people feel guilty or defensive. Moral courage means standing behind your principles, not using them to try and convert others.

RESOLVING ETHICAL DILEMMAS

How to make difficult choices

Life is full of tough choices. For guidance, we might defer to religious teachings, or consider the karmic implications: Whom will this affect and how? Even then, some dilemmas may seem insoluble, especially those involving life-or-death matters or conflicting obligations. How do we tackle knotty problems?

An elderly aunt whose care I'm in charge of has made me promise that no extreme measures will be used to prolong her life. Am I wrong to go along with this? When the time comes should I do whatever possible to keep her alive, even if she's on life support?

The dilemma we face in a situation like this is compounded by the difficulty we have in knowing exactly what others would want. No matter how empathic you are, when you look into the face of a dying person you invariably ask yourself: Who am I to play God and determine her fate? How do I know what she's really feeling right now? Despite what our loved ones say when they're healthy, as death approaches they may have a change of heart and put up a fight. On the other hand, there are terminally ill people in so much pain and distress that they literally beg their caregivers to help them die. Your obligation is to honor the wishes of your aunt, regardless of your own beliefs about end-of-life issues.

But how will I know her wishes?

So that you and your aunt's doctors will not have to guess, have her put her instructions in writing while she's still in full command of her faculties. In those instances when it's too late to get clear instructions from someone who's dying, do your best to recall how the person has approached the big questions in the past: What religious or ethical convictions did she espouse? What beliefs about the afterlife? What fears or concerns about death? If you can stay focused on helping your loved one make this sacred transition, you won't get sidetracked into ethical debates.

All this talk about dying has made me think about organ donation. How does donating organs affect the karma of the donor and the recipient?

Nearly every faith tradition sanctions organ donation, albeit to differing degrees. Though Judaism forbids desecration of the body and requires that every part of it must be buried, in certain circumstances it is considered a great *mitzvah*—act of charity—to donate an organ to save another's life. The donation must be made to meet a specific need, however. Simply donating an organ to an organ bank or a medical school is forbidden. Islam, too, has an injunction against body mutilation but deems saving a life more important and allows organ donation.

Whether you give someone an organ—a kidney, say—while you're still alive, or make provisions to

> **"** As soon as you
> **trust yourself,**
> you will know how to live. **"**
>
> JOHANN WOLFGANG VON GOETHE
> (1749–1832)

donate organs after your death, this is a generous and compassionate gesture that will most likely bring positive karma to both donor and recipient. However, you should be clear about your intentions. Are you donating the organ freely, or have you been pressured by another person or public opinion? If you're uncomfortable with the notion of donating organs, then don't tick the donor box on your driver's license or schedule surgery to give your cousin your kidney. Overriding your instincts invites negative karma.

How does abortion affect karma? My friend just found out she's pregnant and is planning to terminate, though I can tell she's agonizing over the decision. In her heart she feels it's the right thing to do, but she needs to come to terms with it and find a way to deal with her sense of loss. What can she do so she won't have to carry a heavy burden of sadness and negative karma?

No one takes abortion lightly. Most religions oppose it as a general practice. Even women with no religious convictions against the procedure generally experience feelings of grief and loss. A spiritual practice can provide solace and support, so long as the woman isn't paralyzed with guilt over breaking a precept of her faith.

For many women, creating some sort of ceremony or ritual is a good way to acknowledge the gravity of the decision to abort while allowing them to let go and move on. Some Eastern teachings hold that abortion brings bad karma to the fetus by preventing the soul from incarnating and working off karma from its previous lifetimes. In Japan, where abortion is common, a woman might hold a memorial service for her aborted fetus during which she would make offerings to Jizo Bodhisattva, protector of travelers and children, to watch over the aborted soul until its rebirth.

At times it seems easier to deal with big issues like abortion and euthanasia than to handle more mundane dilemmas. For example, the other day while I was antiques shopping with a friend and her five-year-old son, the boy broke a vase. His mother quickly walked away and pretended she hadn't seen. I was in a quandary about what to do: Should I let her know I saw what happened and encourage her to inform the shopkeeper? If she refused, should I tell the shopkeeper myself? Or should I stay out of the matter altogether, on the grounds that it's her kid and her problem? What's my obligation in a situation like this?

BASICALLY, YOU'RE ASKING WHETHER YOUR LOYALTY SHOULD BE TO FRIENDSHIP OR TO WHAT'S RIGHT. THOSE ARE NOT MUTUALLY EXCLUSIVE.

The first step would be to take the mother aside and tell her what you saw. Maybe she really wasn't aware of what her son had done. If she showed concern and rushed to inform the shopkeeper, then your job would be done. It would be up to the two of them to sort it out.

ff Sages say that the path
of wisdom is narrow and
difficult to tread, as narrow
as the edge of a razor. **JJ**

UPANISHADS (c.600 BCE)

But what if she denied everything—maybe even got mad at me for making accusations about her son?

It might be tempting to march up to the shopkeeper and recount every detail of what happened, but you'd probably only end up in a her-word-against-yours shouting match. That would resolve nothing and would leave everyone mistrustful and angry.

Instead of escalating tensions, why not appeal to your friend's maternal instincts? Ask if she would really want to set a bad example for her child by sending the message that it's OK to destroy other people's property and not own up to what you've done. You might even add that sidestepping responsibility would be bad for her karma and her child's. If she still was not convinced, you could tell her you're sorry, she left you no choice but to speak to the shopkeeper yourself. That might put a crimp in your friendship for a while, but if your relationship had any substance to it, you'd eventually be able to patch things up.

But wouldn't it be bad for my karma to intervene?

You should intervene only as a last resort. The point is not to judge your friend but to set things right. Neither you nor she would be able to predict the shopkeeper's response. Most storeowners carry insurance and factor a certain amount of breakage or loss into their overhead. If the item was not too expensive and your friend was straightforward about the accident, the shopkeeper might even waive the charge. On the other hand, if the boy had just pulverized a $12,000 Ming vase there might be some hefty damages to pay. That would undoubtedly teach your friend to keep a closer eye on her child and not take him places where there's a good chance he might break something.

Further Reading

ROBERT AITKEN
*The Mind of Clover: Essays in
Zen Buddhist Ethics*
North Point Press, 1984

ARISTOTLE
The Nichomachean Ethics
Oxford University Press, 1998

ANNIE WOOD BESANT
Karma
Theosophical Publishing House,
1975

SWAMI PRABHAVANANDA and
CHRISTOPHER ISHERWOOD,
trans.
*The Bhagavad-Gita: The Song
of God*
Signet Classics, 2002

SIMON BLACKBURN
*Being Good: A Short Introduction
to Ethics*
Oxford University Press, 2003

H. P. BLAVATSKY
The Secret Doctrine
Quest Books, 1993

MARY T. BROWNE
*The Power of Karma: How to
Understand Your Past and Shape
Your Future*
HarperCollins, 2002

PAUL BRUNTON
What Is Karma?
Larson, 1998

PAUL CARUS
Karma: A Story of Buddhist Ethics
Kessinger, 2004

RANDY COHEN
*The Good, the Bad & the
Difference: How to Tell Right
from Wrong in Everyday
Situations*
Broadway, 2002

RABBI DAVID A. COOPER
*God Is A Verb: Kabbalah and the
Practice of Mystical Judaism*
Riverhead, 1997

THE DALAI LAMA
Ethics for the New Millennium
Riverhead, 2001

V. HANSON, R. STEWARD, and
S. NICHOLSON, eds.
*Karma: Rhythmic Return to
Harmony*
Quest Books, 1990 (3rd ed.)

PETER SINGER
*How Are We to Live?: Ethics in an
Age of Self-Interest*
Prometheus, 1995

RUDOLF STEINER
René Querido, ed.
*A Western Approach to
Reincarnation and Karma:
Selected Lectures and Writings*
Steiner Books, 1977

ROBERT THURMAN
*Infinite Life: Seven Virtues for
Living Well*
Riverhead, 2004

*The Tibetan Book of the Dead: The
Great Liberation Through
Hearing in the Bardo*
FRANCESCA FREEMANTLE and
CHÖGYAM TRUNGPA, trans.
and commentary
Shambhala, 2002

PANDIT RAJMANI TIGUNAIT, Ph.d.
*From Death to Birth: Understanding
Karma and Reincarnation*
Himalayan Institute Press, 1997

SWAMI PRABHAVANANDA and
FREDERICK MANCHESTER,
trans.
*The Upanishads: Breath of the
Eternal*
Signet Classics, 2002

RUTH WHITE
Karma and Reincarnation
Weiser, 2001

HSING YUN
*Being Good: Buddhist Ethics for
Everyday Life*
Weatherhill, 1998

References

INTRODUCTION

p. 6 "Was it something …?" "Bad Karma," written and recorded by Warren Zevon, from *Sentimental Hygiene*, Zevon Music Inc./BMI, 1987.

p. 6 "Ain't no running …" "Karma," written by Will Adams, Allan Pineda, Nigel Harrison, and Deborah Harry, and recorded by the Black Eyed Peas, from *Behind the Front*, Interscope, 1998.

p. 6 "There's something to be said …" *My Name Is Earl*, NBC-TV.

p. 7 "four unconjecturables" *Acintita Sutta, Anguttara Nikaya* IV.77.

p. 9 "When a man …" The Talmud, Shabbat 31a.

p. 13 "our life is …" Reginald A. Ray, *Buddhist Tantra: Teachings and Practices for Touching Enlightenment with the Body*, CD set, Sounds True.

DIALOGUE 1: TRADITIONAL WISDOM

p. 15 "Karma provides the stimulus …" *The Encyclopedia of Eastern Philosophy and Religion*, Shambhala, 1986, p. 175.

p. 16 "Where a man sows …" Galatians 6: 7–9, *The Jerusalem Bible*, Doubleday, 1968.

p. 16 "Whatever I do …" *Upajjhatthana Sutta, Anguttara Nikaya* V: 57.

p. 17 "Whatever is in his mind …" *Bhagavad-Gita* VIII.6, *The Bhagavad Gita: The Ethics of Decision-Making*, translated with commentary by Antonio T. de Nicolàs, Nicholas-Hays, 2004.

p. 17 three types of karma Sri Swami Sivananda, "Karma Yoga," www.dlshq.org/teachings/karma yoga.htm; "Karma/Kamma–The Laws of Cause and Effect," www.the nazareneway.com/karma.htm

p. 18 "We are at liberty …" Ven. Mahasi Sayadaw, "The Theory of Karma," www.buddhanet.net/e-learning/karma.htm

p. 21 "the unerring Law of Retribution" H. V. Blavatsky, *The Secret Doctrine*, Vol. 1, Book 3, Chapter 16, Theosophical Society online edition, www.theosociety.org/pasadena/sd/sd1-3-16.htm

p. 21 "You cannot do wrong …" Ralph Waldo Emerson, *Compensation*, from *Essays: First Series*, reprint of 1904 edition, AMS, 1979, pp. 110, 116.

DIALOGUE 2: RESPONSIBILITY

p. 27 "Sometimes the flow from the past …" Thanissaro Bhikkhu, "Karma," www.accesstoinsight.org/lib/authors/thanissaro/karma.html

DIALOGUE 3: INTENTION

p. 33 "Not all good intentions …" Thanissaro Bhikkhu, "The Road to Nirvana Is Paved with Skillful Intentions," www.accesstoinsight.org/lib/authors/thanissaro/karma.html

p. 37 "Happy is the person …" *Ten Eternal Questions: Wisdom, Insight and Reflection for Life's Journey*, edited by Zoë Sallis, Duncan Baird Publishers, 2005, p. 117.

DIALOGUE 4: SELF-AWARENESS

p. 45 "The man who is aware of himself …" Virginia Woolf, Chapter 6: "Montaigne," in *The Common Reader: First Series*, eBooks@Adelaide, 2004, http://etext.library.adelaide.edu.au/w/woolf/virginia/w91c/chapter6.htm

DIALOGUE 5: EMOTIONS

p. 49 "We only become …" *Destructive Emotions: How Can We Overcome Them?*, a dialogue with the Dalai Lama narrated by Daniel Goleman, Bantam Books, 2003, p. 132.

p. 50 "The more you look at anger …" *Destructive Emotions*, p. 81.

p. 52 "Anger is a sign …" Mark Epstein, MD, "How to Use Anger," *O: The Oprah Magazine*, October 2002, p. 124.

p. 53 "ability to absorb their anger …" Eric Goldscheider, "Peace Pagoda Grounds a Buddhist Group in New England," *The New York Times*, October 1, 2005, Sec. B, p. 5.

DIALOGUE 6: THOUGHTS

p. 55 "Never suffer a thought …" Thomas Jefferson, letter to his grandson Francis Wayles Eppes, May 21, 1816, *The Family Letters of Thomas Jefferson*, edited by Edwin Morris Betts and James Adam Bear, Jr., University of Missouri Press, 1966, p. 415

p. 58 the way to control a cow

Shunryu Suzuki, *Zen Mind, Beginner's Mind*, Weatherhill, 1973, p. 32.

p. 59 "staring back" Matthieu Ricard in *Destructive Emotions: How Can We Overcome Them?*, a dialogue with the Dalai Lama narrated by Daniel Goleman, Bantam Books, 2003, p. 214.

p. 61 "As [a man] thinketh …" Proverbs 23:7, The Bible, King James version.

DIALOGUE 7: INTIMACY

p. 71 Remember (or imagine) Robert Thurman, *Infinite Life: Seven Virtues for Living Well*, Riverhead, 2004, pp. 23–4.

DIALOGUE: 8 HONESTY

p. 73 "Raurava hell" *Markandeya Purana* X:58, pp. 80–4; also see Sri Swami Sivananda, "Lokas or Planes: Karmas and Hells," in *What Becomes of the Soul After Death* www.experiencerestival.com/raurava

p. 73 "Let your conduct be marked …" *Taittiriya Upanishad* I.11.1, in *The Upanishads: Breath of the Eternal*, translated by Swami Prabhavananda and Frederick Manchester, Signet Classics, 2002, p. 54.

p. 73 Saint Augustine … declared all lies Sissela Bok, *Lying: Moral Choice in Public and Private Life*, Vintage, 1979, p. 35.

p. 73 even a justifiable lie … *Ambalatthikarahulovada Sutta, Majjhima Nikaya* 61.

p. 74 "When in doubt, tell the truth … remember

anything," Mark Twain, *Mark Twain's Notebook*, 1894, *The Complete Works of Mark Twain*, Vol. 1, Harper, 1925, pp. 237, 240.

p. 79 questions Randy Cohen Randy Cohen, *The Good, the Bad, & the Difference*, Broadway Books, 2002, p. 170.

p. 80 Lies not only break the trust Sissela Bok, *Lying*, p. 25.

p. 81 "You may modify …" The Talmud, Yebamot 65b.

DIALOGUE 9: GIVING

p. 83 websites with donor information: newtithing.org; www.justgive.org; www.networkforgood.org

p. 85 Giving only what you don't want … "kingly" or "queenly" giving "The Gift That Cannot Be Given," Q & A with Marcia Rose, *Tricycle: The Buddhist Review*, Summer 2003, p. 38; "Dana: The Practice of Giving," edited by Bhikkhu Bodhi, www.accesstoinsight.org/lib/authors/various/wheel367.html; Bhikkhu Yogavacara Rahula, "Practicing Dhamma in Everyday Life: Generosity," www.bhavanasociety.org

pp. 85–6 Maimonides … become self-reliant Julie Salamon, *Rambam's Ladder: A Meditation on Generosity and Why It Is Necessary to Give*, Workman, 2003, p. 7.

p. 86 Charity is one … for the less fortunate The Koran 2:177, 2:261–6; 3:92; www.islamicbulletin.org/howto htm.htm; Maulana Wahiduddin Khan, "The Concept of Charity

in Islam," www.alrisala.org/Articles/mailing_list/charity.html

p. 88 endow a prize Robert Strauss, "Honor Thy Father," *The New York Times*, Education Life, July 31, 2005, p. 12.

p. 88 Every year, three scholarship students Murray Rosenthal, DDS, personal communication.

DIALOGUE 10: TAKING AND RECEIVING

p. 91 "All stealing …" Ralph Waldo Emerson, "Experience," *Essays: Second Series*, 1844, *The Complete Works of Ralph Waldo Emerson*, Vol. III, www.rwe.org

DIALOGUE 11: WEALTH

p. 103 "The love of money …" 1 Timothy 6:10, The Bible, King James Version.

p. 103 "the mutual rivalry …" The Koran 102:1.

p. 103 Seek wisdom The Doctrine and Covenants of the Church of Jesus Christ of the Latter-Day Saints 6:7.

DIALOGUE 12: RIGHT LIVELIHOOD

p. 106 "scheming …" *Maha-cattarisaka Sutta, Majjhima Nikaya* 117.

p. 106 not to engage … poison *Vanijja Sutta, Anguttara Nikaya* V.177.

DIALOGUE 13: WELL-BEING

p. 111 many causes and conditions Sharon Salzberg, personal communication.

p. 112 mindfulness meditation … enhances

immune function Richard J. Davidson, PhD, Jon Kabat-Zinn, PhD, et al, "Alternations in Brain and Immune Function Produced by Mindfulness Meditation," *Psychosomatic Medicine*, Vol. 65, 2003, pp. 564–70.

pp. 113–4 forgiving Christina M. Pulchalski, MD, "Forgiveness, Spiritual and Medical Implications," *The Yale Journal for Humanities in Medicine*, September 2002; The Kentucky Forgiveness Collective www.uky.edu/~ldesh2/latest.htm; Stanford Forgiveness Project www.forgiving.org

DIALOGUE 14: COLLECTIVE KARMA

p. 124 "We're all in this together ..." one-woman show, "The Search for Signs of Intelligent Life in the Universe," written by Jane Wagner, Harper Paperback, 1991.

p. 125 universality principle Immanuel Kant, *Groundwork of the Metaphysics of Morals*, Cambridge University Press, 1998, and *Kant: The Metaphysics of Morals*, Cambridge University Press, 2nd rev. ed., 1996.

DIALOGUE 15: CONNECTION

p. 127 take a pet's life ... shelter Randy Cohen, *The Good, the Bad, & the Difference* p. 253.

p. 128 "There is not a single creature ..." John Daido Loori, "Just the Right Amount," *Tricycle: The Buddhist Review*, Winter 1992.

p. 130 "We need to approach our personal technologies ..." Christine Rosen, "Bad Connections," *The New York Times Magazine*, March 20, 2005, p. 19.

pp. 132–3 "profound courtesy ... creation" "ADAB: All Good Traits Combined," interview with Andrew Harvey by Frederic A. Brussat, *Spirituality & Health*, www.spiritualityhealth.com

DIALOGUE 16: DOING GOOD

p. 135 "the welfare of the world" *Bhagavad-Gita* III.20, 25, in *Hindu Scriptures*, translated and edited by R. C. Zaehner, Everyman's Library, 1992.

p. 141 do what is necessary ... example to others *Bhagavad-Gita*, III.3–9, 19–26.

pp. 142–3 A karmic encounter With appreciation to Jennifer and Steven Lamb of Stamford, Connecticut.

DIALOGUE 17: KARMIC PAYBACK

p. 149 restorative justice U.S. Department of Justice Online Restorative Justice Notebook, www.ojp.usdoj.gov/nij/rest-just/ch1.htm; Prison Fellowship International, Restorative Justice online, www.restorativejustice.org; Restorative Justice Consortium, www.restorativejustice.org.uk

DIALOGUE 18: CLEARING BAD KARMA

p. 151 "A Buddhist who is fully convinced ..." Ven.

Mahasi Sayadaw, "Theory of Karma in Buddhism," www.buddhanet.net/t_karma.htm

p. 151 "work creatively ..." Reginald A. Ray, "The Practice of Karma," *Shambhala Sun Online*, March 2002, www.shambhalasun.com/Archives/Columnists/Ray/mar_02.htm

p. 152 "description of our personality ..." Paul R. Fleischman, MD, and Forrest D. Fleischman, "Karma and Chaos," in *Karma and Chaos: New and Collected Essays on Vipassana Meditation*, Vipassana Research Publications, 1999, p. 114. Also at www.pariyatti.com/kc.pdf

p. 153 "Buddhism teaches ..." Reginald A. Ray, "The Practice of Karma."

DIALOGUE 20: KARMIC CONUNDRUMS

p. 166 Jizo Bodhisattva William LaFleur, "The Cult of Jizo: Abortion Practices in Japan and What They Can Teach the West," *Tricycle: The Buddhist Review*, Summer 1995, p. 41.

Index

Acknowledgments

Endless gratitude to Bob Saxton, editorial director of Duncan Baird Publishers, who conceived the idea of a dialogue-based "How to" series and with unfailing patience and humor shepherded *Good Karma*—and its predecessor, *Happiness*—through the editing process. Thanks to Dan Sturges of DBP for the handsome book design, and to Duncan Baird for his ongoing support. One could not be blessed with a more gracious and accommodating publishing team.

A deep bow to: Sharon Salzberg for insight on karma from a Buddhist perspective; David Nichtern for input on karma and intimacy; Barbara Grande, LCSW, for observations on everyday ethics; Hasan Asif, MD, for psycho-spiritual wisdom; Andrew Harvey for inspiration and source material. Special thanks to Jennifer and Steven Lamb, bodhisattvas of transportation, for the karmic encounter on pp. 142–3.